GREAT FLOWERING
LANDSCAPE SHRUBS

GREAT FLOWERING
LANDSCAPE SHRUBS

Vincent A. Simeone, Photographs by Bruce Curtis
Foreward by Micheal D. Coe
Introduction by Michael A. Dirr

 Ball Publishing | Batavia, Illinois

Ball Publishing
P.O. Box 9
335 N. River St.
Batavia, IL 60510
www.ballpublishing.com

Library of Congress Cataloging-in-Publication Data

Simeone, Vincent A.

  Great flowering landscape shrubs / Vincent A. Simeone ; photographs by
Bruce Curtis ; foreword by Michael D. Coe ; introduction by Michael A. Dirr.
     p. cm.
  Includes bibliographical references and index.
  ISBN 1-883052-42-4 (hardcover : alk. paper)
  1. Ornamental shrubs. 2. Landscape gardening. I. Title.

  SB435.S483 2005
  635.9'76--dc22

                    2004029016

Printed and bound in China by Imago.
10 09 08 07 06 05 04 1 2 3 4 5 6 7 8 9

ISBN 1-883052-42-4

Special Thanks

A special thank you to various gardens and nurseries that allowed us to photograph a wide variety of shrubs: Bayard Cutting Arboretum, Environmentals Nursery, Martin Viette Nursery, Planting Fields Arboretum State Historic Park, and The Walt Whitman Birthplace.

} "Yet my friend could not fail to perceive that

the creation of a Landscape-Garden offered

to the true muse the most magnificent

of opportunities. Here was, indeed, the

fairest field for the display of invention,

or imagination, in the endless combining

of forms of novel Beauty."

— **Edgar Allan Poe**

Table of Contents

Acknowledgments

This book would not have been possible without the support of my many talented colleagues, friends, and family. Their encouragement and unconditional support has been inspiring. I am fortunate enough in my horticultural career to have many positive influences including the guidance of two legendary plantsmen, Dr. Michael A. Dirr and Dr. Allan M. Armitage. I also owe a great deal of gratitude to Irene Virag, who evoked in me a passion for garden writing.

Most important, I would like to dedicate this book to W. R. Coe and his wife, Mai Rogers, for their admiration for horticulture and the creation of one of the most uniquely beautiful places on earth, now known as Planting Fields Arboretum State Historic Park.

Foreword

Since the early 1920s, Planting Fields Arboretum has been a showplace for specimen trees, beautiful gardens, and masses of unique and choice flowering shrubs. This former estate turned public garden offers one of the most comprehensive collections of woody plants available in the Northeast.

My grandfather William Robertson Coe (WRC in this essay) was born in England in 1869, moved to this country with his family in 1883, and never forgot his English roots. When he acquired Planting Fields in 1913, he set about to recreate an English country estate in his adopted land.

When the Coes moved to Oyster Bay, this property looked nothing like what it does today. My grandfather immediately hired distinguished landscape designers Lowell and Sargent, who were succeeded by the Olmsted Brothers, to tackle the mammoth task of transforming disorder into order and converting wilderness and farmland into the semblance of an English landscape.

WRC and his wife, Mai, adored rhododendrons and azaleas, as did their oldest son, Bill (my father), and they began purchasing many hundreds of rare and beautiful specimens from West Coast growers. But the jewel in the crown as far as my grandfather's acquisition of shrubs for Planting Fields is the estate's great and unique collection of hybrid camellias. The story begins with the visit to Planting Fields by Gomer Waterer, of the well-known and still-flourishing firm John Waterer & Sons of Berkshire, England. Mr. Waterer informed my grandfather that the firm maintained a collection of hybrid camellias on the Isle of Guernsey, and this stimulated WRC to place a large order from them. However, being a horticultural tyro, he had no idea that these camellias were not hardy: Guernsey, in the midst of the English Channel, does not undergo the frigid winters so typical of the northeastern United States.

The camellias having arrived, WRC innocently asked Roland Sargent, his landscape gardener, where to put them. To Coe's surprise, Sargent replied that they would have to go in their own greenhouse. So, in a remarkably short time, Planting Fields' Camellia Greenhouse was designed and built to house them. Today, a visit to the camellia collection during the winter months is one of the high points of a Planting Fields tour. Ironically, Planting Fields now features a hardy camellia collection on the grounds surrounding the greenhouse.

WRC took an immense pleasure in what he had created at Planting Fields. He and Mai, and, after her death, his third wife, Caroline, were in residence there during the autumn, late spring, and early summer months, during which my grandfather took long walks every fine day through his domains, accompanied by the superintendent. He was a collector of superior flowering shrub varieties, fine specimen trees, and unusual greenhouse collections. He knew every specimen tree and every shrub individually and by its proper Latin name.

Today, Planting Fields continues to feature some of the most select varieties of flowering shrubs available. Visitors can enjoy many older varieties of shrubs that have helped to shape the American landscape, as well as new and exciting hybrids that are ideal for the home garden. One significant and more modern feature of the arboretum is the Synoptic Garden, which is a collection of superior flowering shrubs arranged in alphabetical order by scientific name. This living library allows homeowners to learn about the virtues of these exceptional garden favorites.

Michael D. Coe
Chairman, Planting Fields Foundation

Introduction

This wonderful new book, *Great Flowering Landscape Shrubs,* combines the best of the older cultivars with the newest of the new. Each major plant group, for example *Buddleia,* butterfly bush, includes its characteristics, care, culture, and nuances. This textual treatment sets the landscape table for the gardener who can then forage far afield in search of the newer cultivars that the author describes. What distinguishes this garden treatise from its brethren is the easy readability and integrity of the information. Written by a gardener and plantsman, the book upgrades and extends the standard fare offered in similarly themed books. The presentation carries the reader into the twenty-first century by featuring the newer, available cultivars. If names like 'Bumblebee', 'Rose Creek', 'Attraction', 'Silver Frost', 'Sixteen Candles', 'Jim's Pride', and 'Alice' do not ring the garden bells, the reason is newness to commerce.

Vinnie (Mr. Simeone) has produced a terrific mini-treatise on flowering shrubs that educates, inspires, and promotes acquisition. The book transcends the norm and moves new shrub cultivars into the twenty-first century.

Michael A. Dirr
Department of Horticulture
University of Georgia

A Brief Introduction to Flowering Shrubs

Flowering shrubs shape the backbone of the landscape, offering a rich palette of textures, colors, and forms. Each shrub can provide a diverse selection of ornamental features such as foliage, flowers, fruit, and bark texture. They can also offer year-round interest when effectively combined with herbaceous plants and other desirable garden treasures. A well-designed garden possesses a balanced mixture of plants that will provide a succession of horticultural interest throughout the year. While this tends to intimidate beginner gardeners, there is really no mystery to gardening with flowering shrubs. If used correctly, flowering shrubs will provide years of enjoyment in the garden and will enhance other plantings such as perennials, vines, and trees.

The exceptional shrubs offered in this book have been chosen with careful consideration of a number of important characteristics. These selective standards include ornamental value, cultural adaptability, pest resistance, and function in the landscape. All of these factors have a considerable influence on the viability of the plant in the horticultural community. Superior varieties of shrubs that are both attractive and versatile are steadily gaining in popularity on the retail market.

This book celebrates the rebirth of many traditional garden favorites and also gazes into the future with the introduction of new, innovative shrub selections. Many of the popular flowering shrubs known as "old-fashioned" shrubs have recently regained popularity in American gardens. These common shrubs were popular during the first half of the twentieth century. Plants such as hydrangeas, lilacs, butterfly bushes, viburnums, and weigelas are now being reintroduced and selected for improved flowers and fruit, better pest resistance, and compact growth habits more suitable for residential sites. This new breed of plants requires less maintenance and offers superior horticultural interest for an extended period of time.

The plant diversity available to home gardeners is steadily increasing. Although flowering shrubs are often thought of as spring bloomers, many shrubs also bloom in the summer and fall months. More than ever, flowering shrubs provide multiseason interest. For example, glossy abelia *(Abelia x grandiflora)* blooms in the northeastern United States from June until the first hard frost in October. The red fall foliage and star-shaped flower stalks that persist after the flowers fade provide added fall and early winter interest. Many consider viburnums the nobility of garden shrubs and are cherished for their unsurpassed beauty and versatility in the landscape. Depending on the species chosen, these prized shrubs frequently provide three seasons of interest, with spring or summer blooms, excellent rich green foliage, ornamental fruit, and brilliant fall foliage color. Similarly, while hydrangeas have been largely overlooked over the past few decades, in recent years hundreds of exciting species and new varieties now blanket local garden centers, nurseries, and public gardens. Hydrangea varieties are now available in a rainbow of shapes, colors, and sizes to accommodate almost any garden situation.

With so many outstanding shrubs available today, home gardeners have numerous possibilities in creating the perfect landscape. Whether your goal is to establish a colorful shrub border, functional foundation planting, or simple mass planting, incorporating flowering shrubs into the landscape is essential. Flowering shrubs present gardeners with endless opportunities in an ever-changing garden environment.

Shrubs Defined

A shrub is defined as a woody plant that is smaller than a tree and usually multistemmed, producing branches from or near the base. There are three basic types of shrubs—evergreen, semi-evergreen, and deciduous. Evergreen shrubs are shrubs that retain their leaves year-round. Rhododendrons are popular flowering evergreens found in many gardens today. Semi-evergreen shrubs retain at least part of their foliage throughout the year. On occasion in unusually cold winters, semi-evergreens will become deciduous. Glossy abelia is a good example of a semi-evergreen shrub in northern climates. A deciduous shrub will shed its leaves in the autumn and regain them in spring. Forsythia is characterized as a deciduous flowering shrub.

USING PLANT NAMES

Both scientific plant names and common names are used to distinguish shrubs. They are a vital part of our daily gardening routine. Systematically, all plants are classified by a system known as binomial nomenclature. This two-name system developed by Carl Linnaeus, a Swedish naturalist, scientifically names and classifies plants. Scientific names are written in Latin, which, in plant terms, is an international language accepted around the world. These scientific names are comprised of a genus, also referred to as generic term, and a specific epithet. A genus is defined as a group of closely related plants comprising one or more species. The second name, a specific epithet, identifies the specific member of a genus. Collectively, the two names represent the particular species. For example, the scientific name for oak leaf hydrangea is Hydrangea quercifolia.

Although binomial nomenclature may be intimidating to the casual gardener, scientific names are an essential part of the gardening world. Many gardeners prefer to use the common names of plants because they tend to be more user-friendly to the novice. However, there are several drawbacks of using common names exclusively. First, common names are not agreed upon worldwide, as are scientific names. Instead, common names are usually accepted regionally to represent plants growing in a particular area or environment. Second, a particular plant may have several common names, making it difficult to verify what the plant is. For example, *Pieris japonica* is known as andromeda or Japanese pieris. But the use of the name andromeda could cause confusion given that there is a separate genus named *Andromeda* as well. Common names often describe unique characteristics

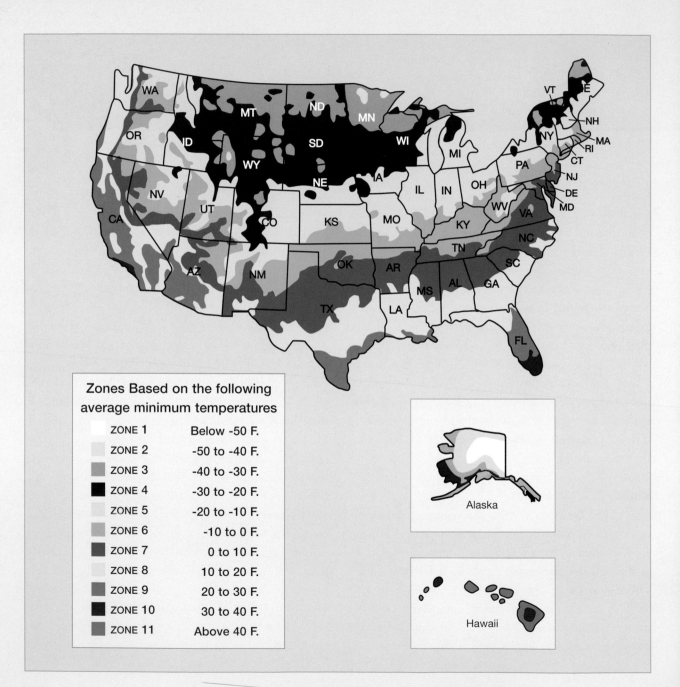

Zones Based on the following average minimum temperatures

	Zone	Temperature
	ZONE 1	Below -50 F.
	ZONE 2	-50 to -40 F.
	ZONE 3	-40 to -30 F.
	ZONE 4	-30 to -20 F.
	ZONE 5	-20 to -10 F.
	ZONE 6	-10 to 0 F.
	ZONE 7	0 to 10 F.
	ZONE 8	10 to 20 F.
	ZONE 9	20 to 30 F.
	ZONE 10	30 to 40 F.
	ZONE 11	Above 40 F.

Alaska

Hawaii

HARDINESS ZONE MAP

The USDA Plant Hardiness Zone Map is designed to illustrate the average minimum temperatures of the United States. The map is separated into eleven zones, 1 representing the coldest Zone and 11 representing the warmest zone. Although there are other environmental factors that impact plant adaptability—such as heat, humidity and rainfall—cold hardiness is one of the most important factors influencing plant survival. To use the map, identify the area on the map where you live. There will be a zone number assigned to that region. For example, the hardiness zone for Chicago is Zone 5. For exact temperature ranges within a given hardiness zone, read the zone key located on the right side of the map. It is important to identify the zone where you live to ensure that the plants you select will survive in that climate. Selecting plants that are tender or marginally hardy in any given hardiness zone may result in poor performance or death of the plant. The plant hardiness zone range for each plant species or variety is listed at the end of every plant description.

of plants. For example, summersweet clethra (*Clethra alnifolia*) is native to the East Coast of the United States. Clethra inherited this common name because of its extremely sweet, spicy flower fragrance.

Other important terms that are helpful to know are cultivars, varieties, and hybrids. A cultivar, also known as a cultivated variety, is typically cultivated or selected for certain special attributes that are different than the species. Cultivated varieties are also known as garden varieties. Cultivar names are always capitalized and are typically surrounded by single quotation marks. Instead of single quotations, you may also find single quotes replaced by the letters cv., which represents the term *cultivated variety*. For example, the scientific name for white flowering weigela can be written as *Weigela florida* 'Alba' or *Weigela florida* cv. Alba. The true meaning of the term *variety* is independent from that of a cultivar as it refers to a naturally occurring variation within a species and is always

written in lower case letters and without single quotations. For example, *Viburnum plicatum* var. *tomentosum* is the scientific name for doublefile viburnum. However, for the purpose of this book and unless otherwise specified, the term *notable varieties* listed at the end of each plant description refers to cultivated garden varieties. Bottlebrush buckeye, *Aesculus parviflora* var. *serotina,* is one of a few true natural varieties listed in this book.

Hybrids are simply crosses between different species of plants or sometimes even crosses between two different genera. Horticulturists routinely hybridize plants to create new and exciting plants selections. Most often an x will be located between the genus and specific epithet name represents a hybrid. Common plants, such as roses, are extensively hybridized.

NATIVES VERSUS EXOTIC SPECIES

The purpose of this book is to acknowledge the wonderful attributes of exceptional flowering shrubs that can add beauty and function to the home land-scape. It is not intended to exclude or alienate any group of plants. Recent debate has raised questions about the value and need of native species in the garden and the challenge that invasive exotic species present to our environment. The shrubs listed in this book give equal attention to worthwhile natives and excellent exotic shrubs. There are many worthwhile natives and exotics that are valuable assets to American gardens. The perception that all exotic species are invasive is a false one. It is important to have a diverse landscape that has a strong balance of natives and exotic species. The key to a successful garden and healthy environment is to discourage the infiltration of invasive exotic species whenever possible and to encourage superior natives and noninvasive exotics.

Assorted flowering shrubs in the landscape

Glossy abelia's flowers

Glossy abelia in the landscape

{ *Abelia* spp.
Abelia
Abelia x *grandiflora* (glossy abelia)

Abelia was named after Dr. Clark Abel (1780–1826), a well-known British physician, naturalist, and author. This diverse group of shrubs offers the best of all worlds. With small, trumpetlike white or pink flowers most of the summer and fall, this plant has a reputation as a steady performer. Small, heart-shaped, glossy green leaves turn a brilliant reddish maroon in fall. The arching, graceful growth habit makes abelia ideal for many different landscape situations. Glossy abelia is a highly cultivated flowering shrub ranging in size from 18 in. to 6 ft. in height, depending on the variety you choose.

For best results, plant abelia in moist, well-drained soil and full sun. However, abelia will tolerate poor soils and considerable shade. Abelia blooms on current season's growth, so spring pruning before plants break dormancy is best. Tip pruning can be done to encourage a flush of new leaves and flowers. Selective or occasional rejuvenation pruning will also stimulate flower production.

Abelia is an excellent informal hedge, foundation planting, mass planting, and is also very effective when grouped with herbaceous perennials. Abelia has few pest problems if sited correctly and is an excellent butterfly-attracting plant. Leaves are slow to emerge in the spring, but be patient because abelia will

7

dazzle you from summer until early winter. Hardy from Zones 6–9. Can be treated as a perennial in Zone 5.

NOTABLE VARIETIES

'Bumblebee'. A compact variety with showy lavender-pink flowers.

'Canyon Creek'. Excellent accent plant with new leaves a copper color that fade to yellow and finally green. Foliage turns a bronzy rose color and is quite striking through the fall and winter in moderate climates.

'Confetti'. This attractive variegated selection offers glossy leaves with creamy white edges. As the cooler weather of autumn arrives, beautiful pink tones accent the foliage. The white flowers are also very attractive. This low-growing shrub will form small mounds of colorful growth and is ideal as an accent plant in small groupings. It is a very attractive plant in partial shade.

'Edward Goucher'. A hybrid abelia with lavender-pink flowers and lustrous green leaves turning rich shades of reddish purple in fall. A very popular and widely used variety.

'Francis Mason'. This striking variety has bright yellow leaves that fade to yellow-green with age. This variety also produces light pink flowers but is essentially grown for its foliage. This plant can be effectively used in as an accent plant or in groupings in partial shade.

'Little Richard'. A densely growing variety with masses of small white flowers. The dark, glossy green leaves are quite attractive most of the year.

The golden foliage of *Abelia* 'Francis Mason'

'Rose Creek'. A dwarf selection with rich green leaves during the summer tinged with purple in the autumn. After small, white flowers fade, bright red, star-shaped flower stalks remain through the fall.

'Sherwoodii'. This dense, ground-hugging shrub grows to about 3 ft. tall. A very popular plant for foundation plantings, groupings, and as an edging plant.

Abelia chinensis (Chinese abelia)

Although related to glossy abelia, Chinese abelia is a larger shrub, reaching 7 ft. in height with an equal spread. Leaves are medium green, and small, white trumpet flowers are borne on new growth in profusion. Flowers are fragrant and are smaller than that of glossy abelia. After flowers fade, star-shaped flower stalks remain and change from pale pink to a deep rosy pink.

This Asian species is adaptable to varying light exposure and soils but prefers full sun or partial shade and well-drained, acidic soils.

Chinese Abelia is ideal as a single specimen plant in a shrub border, mass planting, or informal hedge. This tough, cold-hardy flowering shrub grows in Zones 6–9. In Zone 5 it may get killed to the ground and then regenerate from the roots, similar to a herbaceous perennial.

{ *Abeliophyllum distichum*
White forsythia

This close relative of forsythia has noticeable purple flower buds that open to fragrant white, trumpet-shaped flowers in early spring. White forsythia has a graceful, arching growth habit and will grow 3–5 ft. in height with a similar spread. It has medium to dark green leaves with no significant fall coloration. This plant typically sprawls along the ground rather than growing upright. White forsythia will not get nearly as large as its closely related cousin, common forsythia, making it ideal for residential landscapes.

Plants can easily be kept compact and vigorous by pruning the plant down to 12 in. in early spring every few years. White forsythia is adaptable to both acidic and alkaline soils and prefers well-drained soil. For best flowering results, shrubs should be planted in full sun or partial shade.

White forsythia is a low-growing shrub well suited as a low informal hedge, foundation planting, or mass planting, and it will liven up a bland landscape early in the season. It's a very durable plant that will grow in Zones 4–8, but will likely need protection in Zone 4.

{ *Aesculus parviflora*
Bottlebrush buckeye

Bottlebrush buckeye is a choice large-flowering shrub with 12 in. long, white bristly flowers that create a candelabra of color in early summer. The palm-shaped, dark green leaves provide a lush, tropical appearance and transform into a mass of bright yellow in autumn. In late summer, fruit capsules form and disperse smooth, nonedible chestnutlike fruit. The slim, gray, upright-growing stems form dense clumps with plants growing 8–12 ft. tall with a potentially greater spread.

The showy white flowers of bottlebrush buckeye

Bottlebrush buckeye in the landscape

Bottlebrush buckeye is native to the southeastern United States and is one of the most carefree and enjoyable landscape plants available. It prefers moist, well-drained, acidic soil with generous amounts of organic matter and thrives in full sun or partial shade. But this resourceful plant will tolerate various types of soil and considerable shade. Regular pruning is not often needed except in situations where reducing the shrub's size is desired. Pruning the entire plant to 12 in. from the ground will renew this plant back to its floriferous form in one or two seasons. Although bottlebrush buckeye is often grown as a large shrub, frequently the lower limbs are removed to train it into a small tree.

The most important aspect of bottlebrush buckeye to consider is its potential large size. They are excellent whether used as a large shrub or small tree but, regardless, must be given ample room. Bottlebrush buckeye is also very useful in a lawn area, shade garden, or along a woodland path. It is a superb landscape plant that will quickly make your top-ten list of favorite shrubs. Hardy from Zones 4–8; may grow in Zone 9 with proper siting.

A. parviflora var. *serotina* is a naturally occurring variety that blooms later than the species does. Adding both selections to the landscape will ensure weeks of colorful flowers.

Amelanchier spp.
Serviceberry

In general, serviceberry (also known as Juneberry or shadbush) is a large, multistemmed shrub with small bouquets of delicate white flowers in spring. The stems and bark are typically silver or gray. During the fall, the medium to dark green leaves will change to varying shades of yellow, orange, or deep red. One of the most desirable attributes of this plant is the small, blueberry-like fruit, which ripen in early summer. These delicious fruit rank among the best edible treats available. Serviceberries can be used in cooking for pies and preserves, but are most enjoyable when freshly harvested from the plant. A truly scrumptious delight!

As a landscape plant, serviceberry is one of the most adaptable natives, tolerating a vast array of environmental conditions. Plants prefer partial shade in filtered light but will tolerate full sun. While serviceberry is adaptable, moist, well-drained soil is best. As a member of the rose family, several common problems—such as leaf spots, rusts, and powdery mildew—can occur, and the watchful gardener should monitor for pest infestations.

In a garden setting, serviceberry is effective as a specimen plant, in small groupings or mass plantings, and in woodland settings. It can be used to form a dense shrub planting or even be trained as a multi-stemmed small tree. Most landscape species of service-berry reach heights of 15–25 ft. in the landscape and are hardy from Zones 4–9.

Amelanchier laevis (downy serviceberry)

'Cumulus'. A narrow, upright growth habit makes this variety ideal in areas with limited space along walkways and narrow planting areas.

Amelanchier canadensis (shadblow serviceberry)

'Spring Glory'. Somewhat shrubby selection to 10 ft. tall with clusters of white flowers and bright golden orange fall foliage color. Hardy from Zones 3–8.

Amelanchier x *grandiflora* (serviceberry)

'Autumn Brilliance'. The beautiful green summer foliage will turn shades of brilliant red in the fall. The densely arranged gray stems are also attractive during the winter months.

'Ballerina'. The dark green leaves turn bronzy red in the fall. This variety has large, white flower clusters and juicy red fruit that changes to purplish black when ripe. An excellent variety showing good disease resistance.

'Robin Hill'. Pink flower buds unfold to pale pink or white flowers. Lush, green leaves transform from yellow to red in the fall. This variety can easily be trained as a small tree.

{ *Aronia* spp.
Chokecherry

Aronia arbutifolia (red chokecherry)

Red chokecherry is a multistemmed shrub with several worthy features to offer the cultivated garden. Like many plants in the rose family, it has a profusion of beautiful white flower clusters in spring. These small bouquets give way to deep red, glossy fruit, which persist through fall and early winter. The fruit are not edible, and even birds will avoid them because of their sour taste. The shiny, dark green foliage of chokecherry turns bright red or maroon in fall and provides a nice backdrop to the fruit. Red chokecherry will grow 6–10 ft. tall and 3–5 ft. wide.

Chokecherry is very adaptable to varying soil types but prefers well-drained, acidic soil and moderate moisture. However, it is also quite drought tolerant once established and will grow in hot, dry conditions. Full sun is best for maximum flower and fruit production, but partial shade is also acceptable. Selective pruning to remove large, less-productive stems should be done on a regular basis every few years to ensure a continuous healthy crop of productive stems.

This hardy flowering shrub is excellent in mass plantings, small groups, foundation plantings, shade gardens, and it can even be used near the seashore. I have seen this plant perform well in the shade of a woodland garden as well as a highly exposed highway planting. Chokecherry is a very durable and reliable plant that will provide three seasons of interest in your garden. Hardy in Zones 4–9.

'Brilliantissima' is a superior variety with exceptional red/crimson fall color, an abundance of flowers, and larger fruit.

Aronia melanocarpa (black chokecherry)

This species is very similar to red chokecherry, but its fruit is a deep blackish purple. It is an excellent shrub for wet or poorly drained areas of the garden. Hardy to Zone 3.

Buddleia spp.
Butterfly bush
Buddleia davidii (common butterfly bush)

Butterfly bush is a well known flowering shrub attracting a variety of beautiful butterflies into the garden. But in addition to providing a source of food for these lovely creatures, butterfly bush is also one of the most functional and adaptable plants in the landscape.

Butterfly bush is the highlight of the garden during the midsummer and fall season. Its long, spikelike plumes of flowers come in a variety of colors from white to pink to deep purple and even yellow. Flowers are also often fragrant, adding to their list of attributes. The dark green foliage is silver on the undersides, providing a glistening appearance as it waves in the summer winds. The plant will reach a height of 8–10 ft. with a 5–6 ft. spread. Butterfly bush prefers well-drained soils but tolerates poor, rocky, or sandy soils. They do require full sun and do not perform well in shaded areas. Butterfly bush does particularly well in hot, dry conditions. On occasion leafhoppers and spider mites, which are common garden

Butterfly bush in flower

Butterfly feasting on 'Pink Delight' butterfly bush flowers

pests, will feed on butterfly bush, so monitor plants on a regular basis.

Pruning of common butterfly bush is generally done in early spring because flowers are borne on the most current season's growth. Therefore, once a year, a severe pruning to 6–12 in. from the ground is recommended in early spring to stimulate spring and summer growth. This rejuvenation pruning will encourage the plant to produce generous amounts of new flowers. Other species, such as alternate leaf butterfly bush *(Buddleia alternifolia),* which bloom on older growth, should not be pruned in this manner. Instead, modest pruning right after flowering is suggested to keep the plants in shape.

Butterfly bush has many uses in the landscape but is best utilized when combined in perennial borders or in small groupings. Of course, this summer-blooming shrub should be located somewhere in the garden where the flight pattern of butterflies can be easily seen from a patio or window. Some new varieties of butterfly bush are compact and serve well as foundation plantings. Hardy from Zones 5–9.

Many researchers, plant breeders, and horticulturists around the country continue to select superior varieties of butterfly bush. For example, considerable research conducted by Dr. Michael A. Dirr from the University of Georgia, in cooperation with the local nursery and horticultural industry to evaluate butterfly bush species and varieties, has yielded impressive results. From this research several quality selections have been named and introduced into the field. Many other varieties have originated from Europe and other parts of the world.

NOTABLE VARIETIES

Whichever species of butterfly bush you choose, it will undoubtedly enhance the beauty of your garden. This diverse group of flowering shrubs will provide interest in the garden from spring to fall. With a vast array of flower colors, growth habits, and foliage textures, these multipurpose shrubs will add a unique presence in the landscape and also attract beneficial insects.

'Attraction'. This variety forms a medium habit with deep magenta flowers and grayish green foliage. The flowers are quite striking against the lush leaves.

'Black Knight'. One of the darkest flowering forms, with attractive dark purple flowers.

'Harlequin'. This variety seems to be slower growing than the species, and the combination of creamy

Deep purple flowers of *Buddleia* 'Harlequin' with purple coneflower

variegated leaves and deep purple flowers provides nice contrast.

'Lochinch'. A well-known variety that grows into a large, vigorous plant with lavender-blue flowers with orange centers.

'Nanho Blue'. A compact grower with blue flowers and grayish leaves.

'Pink Delight'. One of the largest-flowering forms, with rich pink flowers reaching 12 in long. A real "wow" in the garden.

'Silverfrost'. Another dwarf selection, with white flowers and exceptional silver-gray foliage.

'White Profusion'. This large-growing variety has plumes of white flowers.

Buddleia × weyeriana

This hybrid butterfly bush, known for its unusual golden yellow flowers, possesses very similar landscape characteristics to *Buddleia davidii*. The variety 'Sungold' has golden yellow flowers, and 'Honeycomb'

The unusual yellow flowers of *B. × weyeriana* 'Honeycomb'

is a superior yellow variety with improved foliage and pure yellow flowers that offer a sweet fragrance.

Buddleia alternifolia

This is a less-common species that offers a different appearance in the landscape. The alternate leaf butterfly bush provides a profusion of lilac-purple flower clusters in mid-spring. The arching growth habit and tall stature of the plants (10–15 ft.) present a cascading display of color. The thin, green leaves also provide a fine texture in the landscape. Only modest pruning is recommended after flowering since this species flowers on previous year's wood. Hardy from Zones 5–7.

Buddleia lindleyana

Although more obscure than the other selections mentioned, this is a delightful shrub with small glossy green leaves and purple-violet flowers in summer. Pruning to remove spent flowers is advisable and will usually result in more flowers. Hardy from Zones 7–9.

{ *Callicarpa* spp.
Beautyberry

Beautyberry is a unique shrub that provides a beautiful show late in the season as the cooler temperatures of fall arrive. In the landscape, beautyberry often goes unnoticed because of its generic appearance most of the year. But in late summer and early fall it begins to make its presence known as clusters of small, pink flowers change to glossy purple fruit. By late fall, this amazing shrub provides a spectacular display as the succulent fruit glistens in the autumn sun.

Callicarpa dichotoma (common beautyberry)

Common beautyberry is a compact grower with graceful, arching branches. This small shrub will reach 4 ft. in height with a similar spread. During the summer, soft pink flower clusters open up along each stem. Once the flowers have been pollinated, bunches of

Common beautyberry in fall

bright purple berries emerge along the stems en masse. After the leaves fall off in autumn, the berries become most evident in the garden. The fruit will usually remain on the plants well into late fall until the birds feast on them. Beautyberry is an excellent source of food for several species of songbirds.

Beautyberry performs best in full sun or partial shade. It also likes moist, well-drained soil but is quite adaptable. Selective pruning will keep plants dense and healthy. Occasional rejuvenation pruning can be done in late winter or early spring by cutting plants down to 12 in. This will encourage dense, productive shrubs.

Because of its graceful, cascading growth habit and ornamental fruit, beautyberry is ideal in groups, mass plantings, informal hedges, and foundation plantings. This is a shrub that you want to site in a prominent location in the garden to show it off. The attractive stems bearing fruit can be harvested and used in floral arrangements as well. All species mentioned are hardy from Zones 5–8, except Bodinier beautyberry, which is hardy from Zones 6–8.

NOTABLE VARIETIES

'Albifructus'. This white-fruited form is very showy with milky white fruit that glow in the landscape.

'Early Amethyst'. This early fruiting form produces a profusion of small, lilac colored fruit.

'Issai'. This unique variety sets an abundance of fruit as a young plant providing almost immediate satisfaction.

Callicarpa bodinieri var. *giraldii* (Bodinier beautyberry)

'Profusion' has an upright growth habit reaching 10 ft. in height. The large, dark purple fruit are a stunning addition to the garden. It is ideal for floral arranging since this selection produces the largest fruit of the species and selections mentioned. Leaves emerge a bronze-purple in spring and turn varying shades of purple in fall.

Callicarpa japonica (Japanese beautyberry)

Japanese beautyberry is also a large shrub but has violet-purple fruit. Japanese beautyberry has an upright, graceful, and dense branching structure,

Bodinier beautyberry in winter

making it a very useful garden plant. It can be used as a tall hedge or screening plant. 'Leucocarpa', a white-fruited form, is usually showier than the purple-fruited form.

{ *Calycanthus floridus*
Carolina allspice

This shrub is native to the southeastern United States and is adaptable to many landscape situations. Carolina allspice has large, rich green leaves that turn a golden yellow in fall. The dark, reddish brown flowers, which have many strap-shaped petals, emerge in mid-spring with a distinct fruity fragrance. Although this plant flowers in spring, it will also bloom sporadically through the midsummer months. In fall, unusual urnlike seedpods form and persist through the winter. When dry, the branches and other parts of the plant will emit a camphorlike fragrance.

Carolina allspice is relatively easy to grow. It thrives in full sun or partial shade and prefers moist soils. Selective pruning to remove older stems every few years will keep the plant vigorous. Carolina allspice needs adequate space to grow since it can reach a height of 9 ft. with an equal spread. It will spread by underground stems and colonize the area of the garden where it is growing.

Carolina allspice is suitable in shrub borders, woodland gardens, and mass plantings. It is an excellent choice for heavy, moist soils. Hardy from Zones 4–9.

The deep reddish brown flowers of Carolina allspice

NOTABLE VARIETIES

'Athens'. Rich, lustrous green leaves and unusual yellow flowers. A beautiful and unusual addition to any garden.

Lush foliage of 'Michael Lindsey'

'Michael Lindsey'. Dark green foliage has spinach-like texture turning golden yellow in fall. It offers a beautiful, bold texture in the landscape.

{ *Caryopteris* × *clandonensis*
Bluebeard

Bluebeard is a summer-blooming shrub with slender, blue-green leaves and silvery undersides. The clusters of bright blue flowers grace the garden in late summer. Seed heads form in fall and persist into the winter.

Bluebeard is a low, mounded shrub to about 3 ft. in height. Plants flower on the most current season's growth; therefore, it is beneficial to prune plants down to 8–10 in. in early spring while they are dormant. Although adaptable, bluebeard thrives in full sun and well-drained, moist soils. Once established, this low-maintenance plant is quite drought tolerant.

Bluebeard is ideal in groupings, mass plantings, mixed perennial borders, and foundation plantings.

It is an excellent companion plant to other summer-blooming shrubs such as butterfly bush, St. John's wort, and clethra. Hardy from Zones 6–9.

NOTABLE VARIETIES

'Dark Knight'. Rich, dark blue flowers provide an unusual contrast in the landscape.

'First Choice'. Early blooming form with purple-blue flowers.

'Heavenly Blue'. A well-known variety with a compact growth habit and deep blue flowers.

'Longwood Blue'. A nice selection with blue-violet flowers and a mounded habit.

'Worchester Gold'. An interesting combination of blue flowers and yellow foliage, it offers a nice contrast in the landscape. It is used effectively as an accent plant.

{ *Ceanothus* × *pallidus*
Ceanothus

Ceanothus is a charming, small shrub with glossy, dark green leaves and beautiful, soft pink or blue flowers in early summer. Its unique ornamental characteristics and adaptability make it very versatile in the garden.

Plants will reach a height of about 3 ft. and can grow to be rather bushy. Occasional hand pruning after flowering will keep plants dense and vigorous. In colder climates, plants may be killed to the ground but will likely regenerate from the roots, similar to a perennial. Ceanothus thrives in full sun or partial shade and prefers moist, well-drained soil. This shrub is very user friendly in the garden and can easily be incorporated into perennial borders, rock gardens, foundation plantings, and mass plantings. While it is not commercially popular yet, this plant has real potential in the American landscape garden. Hardy from Zones 7–8 but will possibly grow in Zone 6 in a sheltered location.

NOTABLE VARIETIES

'Marie Simon'. A beautiful variety with soft pink flowers.

'Gloire de Versailles'. The puffs of striking blue flowers make this form very desirable.

{ *Chaenomeles speciosa*
Flowering quince

This old-fashioned shrub has been cultivated for centuries and is now reemerging as a desirable ornamental flowering shrub. Flowering quince is useful in the garden because it can be grown for its aesthetic value or interesting edible fruit. The flowers vary from white to pink to deep red in late winter or early spring, persisting to mid-spring. Flowers are arranged in clusters along the interior of the shrub. The smooth green, applelike fruit ripen in fall and are 2–3 in. in diameter and emit a fruity fragrance. This edible fruit is quite tart and can be cooked to make preserves and jellies. New foliage emerges a bronzy red color and changes to dark, glossy green.

The twigs are often spiny and should to be handled very carefully. Shrubs form a dense thicket of branches and can reach a height of 6–8 ft. in the garden with an equal spread. Flowering quince performs best in full sun and moist, well-drained, acidic soil but is extremely adaptable. Selective pruning can be done in early spring to remove old, unproductive branches. These branches are generally pruned as close to the ground as possible. An alternative is to prune the entire plant done to 6–12 in., which will rejuvenate the plant by stimulating new growth from the base. While this method will revitalize your shrubs, it will take at least a year for the plant to reliably flower and fruit. Light pruning to shape plants can also be done after flowering.

Flowering quince is excellent as a barrier hedge because of its dense, spiny branching pattern. It can also be used in groupings, mass plantings, and in shrub borders. Many gardeners plant it in the garden for early spring interest and to harvest the fruit in the fall. Zones 4–8, and possibly 9 with specific siting.

NOTABLE VARIETIES

'Apple Blossom'. Large, pale pink flowers 2 in. in diameter.

'Cameo'. Double, peachy pink flowers in profusion.

'Toyo-Nishiki'. A unique selection with a combination of white, pink, and red flowers.

{ *Chimonanthus praecox*
Fragrant wintersweet

This delightful winter-blooming shrub will flower in late winter and offers a sweet fragrance at a time when not many plants are blooming in the garden. The small, cup-shaped, waxy yellow flowers with deep reddish purple centers appear as early as December or January in southern gardens and February or March in northern climates,

© Vincent A. Simeone

The bright yellow flowers of fragrant wintersweet

depending on the severity of the winter. Flowers are sensitive to extreme cold temperatures and may be damaged from sudden drops in temperature. The tall, upright habit takes on the form of a small tree and can reach 10–15 ft. high but usually considerably smaller in northern gardens. The dark green, sharply pointed, rough-textured leaves feel like sandpaper when rubbed and turn handsome shades of yellow and green in fall.

Wintersweet is an easy plant to grow in the garden and will adapt to varying types of soils, provided there is adequate drainage. Shrubs flower best in full sun or partial shade in a protected area of the garden. Regular selective pruning to remove older, less productive stems should be done in early spring.

This winter-blooming beauty is excellent as a small specimen, along a wall or near a walkway so the delightful fragrance can be enjoyed by the all who pass by. In addition, branches can be cut and forced into flower indoors for a table centerpiece. Hardy from Zones 6–9.

In Zone 6, this shrub should be located in a protected area of the garden.

{ *Clerodendrum trichotomum*
Harlequin glorybower

This peculiar shrub is one that will dazzle the garden enthusiast late in the growing season. It will go largely ignored much of the year, but in midsummer the showy clusters of fragrant white, tubular flowers emerge, followed by bright blue fruit surrounded by a red, star-shaped shield. The display of flowers and fruit are hard to resist and will stop plant lovers in their tracks. The dark green, fuzzy leaves, when rubbed, smell like peanut butter. Glorybower has a shrubby growth habit and will reach 10 ft. or more in height. However, harsh winters will cause dieback, keeping plants somewhat dwarf. Glorybower will often send up underground shoots, known as suckers, creating a twiggy appearance.

This flowering shrub requires adequate moisture and well-drained soils. It flowers best in full sun but will also perform well in partial shade. Prune in spring to remove deadwood, or selectively prune to reduce size.

Glorybower is most effective when used in combination with other shrubs or herbaceous plants. It will offer late summer and fall interest and makes the perfect complement to summer-blooming plants. Glorybower is hardy from Zones 6–9 but will frequently suffer from dieback in northern climates. In Zone 6, plants may be killed to the ground and regenerate from the base, like herbaceous perennials.

Summersweet clethra in flower

{ *Clethra* spp.

Summersweet
Clethra alnifolia
(summersweet clethra, sweet pepper bush)

Summersweet clethra is a delightful native shrub with mutiseasonal interest and valuable function in the landscape. It grows from New England to the southern United States. In midsummer, spikes of pleasantly fragrant white flowers cover the plant. Flower spikes range in size from 2–6 in. but are typically 5 or 6 in. long on the newer cultivated garden varieties. The lush, deep green leaves change to pale or rich golden yellow in the fall. Interesting seedpods will also form and remain through the winter. Clethra has an upright, spreading growth habit forming a mounded, dense cluster of stems. Plants are fast growing and can reach 4–8 ft. tall with an equal spread.

Summersweet clethra is extremely adaptable, growing from shady woodland settings to sunny seashore conditions. It prefers moist, well-drained soil and full sun or partial shade, but it will tolerate and perform well in many landscapes, both cultivated and natural. In shade it becomes more open and tall growing. Clethra seldom needs pruning but occasional rejuvenation pruning to 6 in. will quickly revive unproductive, leggy plants. Regular selective pruning every few years will also maintain shrubs as dense, productive garden plants.

Clethra is an excellent shrub for mass plantings, foundation plantings, shade gardens, seashore plantings, and informal hedges. It will function as the highlight of the garden or blend into the background. This multipurpose flowering shrub has been highly cultivated over the past few years, making it even more desirable for the home garden. Hardy from Zones 4–9.

NOTABLE VARIETIES

'Compacta'. A very handsome selection with dark green foliage, large white flowers, and a dense, upright growth habit. This plant will grow up to 5 ft. tall with an equal spread. A chance seedling found on a compost pile in New Jersey, this is one of my favorite selections and is worthy of consideration for the home landscape.

'Creel's Calico'. A variegated selection with creamy white speckles on the leaves and white flowers.

'Fern Valley Pink'. A large-flowering, light pink form with an extremely sweet fragrance.

'Hummingbird'. This dwarf selection provides a dense mound of deep green foliage, which turns a golden yellow in fall. This spreading shrub tends to

Five-inch-long flowers of 'Compacta' summersweet

Flowers are not particularly fragrant, as those of summersweet clethra are, but a slight fragrance can be found. The medium to dark green leaves often turn brilliant red or maroon in autumn. Seed clusters turn golden yellow around the same time, adding a nice contrast to the fall foliage coloration. One of the uniquely beautiful attributes of this shrub is the smooth, multicolored, flaking bark. Although this is a four-season characteristic, the bark is most noticeable during the winter months, as it shows up nicely against the background of a freshly fallen snow.

sprawl, making it ideal in herbaceous borders, rock gardens, and foundation plantings.

'Rosea'. This selection was introduced in 1906 and has light pink flowers that fade to white with age.

'Ruby Spice'. Essentially the best pink form with deep, rosy pink flowers that contrast well with the dark green canvas of the foliage.

'September Beauty'. A late-blooming selection flowering about two weeks after most clethra.

'Sixteen Candles'. A seedling of 'Hummingbird', this fine selection offers an extremely dense growth habit and profusion of white flowers that resemble candles on a birthday cake.

Clethra barbinervis (Japanese clethra)

Japanese clethra is quite different from summersweet clethra. It typically grows as a large, upright shrub or small tree to 20 ft. tall. This unique shrub possesses 6 in., elongated clusters of white flowers in midsummer.

© Vincent A. Simeone

Smooth bark of Japanese clethra

© Vincent A. Simeone

Japanese clethra's deep maroon foliage and golden fruit clusters in the fall

Japanese clethra grows best in moist, organic, well-drained soil and full sun or partial shade. If sited in too much shade, flowers and intense fall foliage color will be compromised. Japanese clethra also prefers to be sheltered from intense wind and other harsh conditions.

This large shrub is ideal as a specimen plant for a home landscape and can easily take the place of a dogwood, crabapple, or flowering cherry in a front yard. Hardy from Zones 5–7.

Cornus sericea
Redosier dogwood

While there are many species and varieties of dogwood trees that commonly grow all over the world, there are also several species of shrubby dogwoods that offer merit in the landscape. One of the most common and available shrubby dogwoods is the redosier, or red twig, dogwood, which is native to Eastern Canada and much of the United States. Redosier dogwood is most well known for its bright or deep red stems and branches that are especially colorful during the winter months. In addition, redosier dogwood has an unusual white, flat-topped flower cluster very different from the tree dogwoods. This flat-topped flower cluster, also called a cyme, is borne in late spring or early summer. The large, dark green leaves turn reddish purple in fall. Another ornamental characteristic of this plant is the milky white fruit that ripens in late summer and fall providing a brief display.

Redosier dogwood is extremely adaptable, tolerating many types of soils and conditions. For optimum performance this shrub should be given moist, well-drained soil and full sun or partial shade. It is essential to prune shrubs on a regular basis to encourage the optimum coloration to the stems. Shrubs that are left untouched for many years will lose their stem coloration and form large masses of stems. Selective pruning once a year in the winter or early spring to remove older stems that lack vibrant color will stimulate new growth during the growing season. These stems can be harvested and used for decoration. Stem and leaf diseases may cause a problem with these shrubs, but newer varieties have been developed to resist such problems.

Redosier dogwood is a fast-growing, easy-to-establish shrub that can function in many ways in the home garden. Because it is valued for its colored stems, it is recommended as a mass planting, informal hedge or screen, or as a background to other plants. As mentioned earlier, enthusiastic gardeners can harvest the branches during the holiday season for use in arrangements and decorative displays. Redosier dogwood is extremely cold hardy, growing in Hardiness Zones 2–7, but it does not perform as well in warmer, humid climates.

NOTABLE VARIETIES

'Cardinal'. As the name suggests, it is a superior selection with bright red stems.

'Flaviramea'. The yellow twig dogwood offers striking, golden yellow stems and provides a nice contrast when used with red twig types.

'Silver and Gold'. A variegated type with creamy yellow leaf edges in summer and yellow stems in winter.

There are two other notable varieties from closely related species with garden merit:

C. alba 'Bud's Yellow'. Improved yellow stems and improved disease resistance.

C. sanguinea 'Winter Flame'. A new and unusual variety with tones of yellow, orange, and red in the new stems. Nice fall foliage color with leaves turning a golden yellow and contrasting nicely with the stems. Hardy from Zones 4–7.

{ *Corylopsis* spp.
Winterhazel
Corylopsis pauciflora (buttercup winterhazel)
Although there are many winterhazels native to the Unites States, both species presented here are native to

Rich dark red stems of red twig dogwood

Buttercup winterhazel in flower

Japan. Of the two, buttercup winterhazel is the most compact and suitable for the home landscape with limited space. Winterhazel is well known as an early-blooming shrub with a wide, spreading growing habit. The average size in the garden is 5 ft. tall with a 6–8 ft. spread. This densely growing shrub creates such a thick-branching habit that it is hard to see through it even when it sheds its leaves in the fall. This delicate shrub provides a profuse display of color in the garden that is rivaled by few plants. Buttercup winterhazel has showy yellow, fragrant flowers early in the season, which will persist for several weeks. Flowers appear in late winter or early spring at a time when the garden is just waking up. After the flowers fade, small, pleated green leaves emerge and turn a beautiful golden yellow in the fall.

This unique shrub prefers, moist, organic, acidic, well-drained soil and full fun or partial shade. Pruning should be kept to a minimum, as excessive pruning will disfigure the plant's beautiful growth habit. If the plant is not productive, selective pruning can be done in early spring to encourage new stems that will flower the following year.

Buttercup winterhazel is very effective in woodland gardens, mass plantings, or even as a low screen or informal hedge. Many gardeners underestimate how wide this plant will grow, so remember to give this plant plenty of room. Hardy from Zones 6–8.

Corylopsis spicata (spike winterhazel)

Another native of Japan, spike winterhazel can grow considerably larger than the buttercup winterhazel. Established plants can easily reach 10–12 ft. wide and 8 ft. tall. The dangling, fragrant yellow flowers emerge in mass to provide a spectacular show of early seasonal color. The irregular, zigzagging branching habit offers an artistic pattern during the winter months. After the plant flowers, the new growth emerges tinged with purple before maturing to bluish green. Leaves will turn golden yellow to bronze in the fall. Spike winterhazel is a remarkably easy plant to grow and is often found thriving in moist, shaded areas of the backyard. As with its smaller cousin, buttercup winterhazel, spike winterhazel should receive minimal pruning and be provided with adequate room to grow.

This wide-spreading shrub is excellent in mass plantings, woodland gardens, as a barrier plant, or as a single specimen. Hardy from Zones 5–8.

Cotinus coggygria
Common smokebush

Smokebush is a most unusual looking shrub, with small, hairy, and numerous flowers combining to create what appear to be puffy clouds of smoke. The flower clusters, which can reach 6–8 in. in length and width, can change from various shades of light yellow, pink, and purplish red, depending on the variety you choose. This smoky display occurs in mid to late summer and into the autumn season. The rounded to oval leaves are medium green in summer and turn a yellow-red in fall. However, there are several red- or purple-leafed varieties available that seem to be more popular in the garden world.

Smoky flower clusters of smokebush

and foundation plantings, or as an accent plant. Hardy from Zones 4–8.

NOTABLE VARIETIES

'Grace'. In spring, the new leaves of this unique hybrid unfold pinkish red and mature to blue-green in summer. Leaves turn a deep orange or red in the fall. Very large, smoky clusters of flowers make this plant one of the best varieties available today. This big and bold shrub in the landscape is sure to be the envy of the neighborhood.

'Pink Champagne'. The new growth emerges a bronzy purple, eventually maturing to rich green. Pink, smoky flowers make an impressive display in summer.

'Velvet Cloak'. One of the best purple-leaf varieties with leaves emerging a deep maroon and darkening to purple as they mature. Fall foliage color is rich reddish purple. There is some debate if 'Royal Purple', another widespread variety, is actually the same selection as 'Velvet Cloak'. Both varieties would be excellent choices for the home garden and are commonly found in local garden centers and plant nurseries.

Smokebush is a large shrub, growing to 15 ft. tall with a similar spread, but it can also be maintained as a "cut back" shrub. A "cut back" shrub is maintained by cutting the shrub down to 6–12 in. from the ground in late winter or early spring every year or two. This practice not only keeps the plant more compact, but it also encourages lush, colorful new growth. It is commonly done on the red-leaf varieties such as 'Velvet Cloak' and 'Royal Purple' to encourage new, intensely colored maroon or red leaf shoots each season. Smokebush prefers full sun and well-drained soil but is quite adaptable. It is exceptionally drought tolerant and adaptable to most soil pH ranges and types.

In addition to a "cut back" shrub, smokebush can also be used in a shrub or perennial border, groupings

Cotoneaster spp.
Cotoneaster

Cotoneasters are among the most common and widely used plants in American gardens. There are several shrub and groundcover types that are worthy of mention. Cotoneaster is a medium- to fast-growing plant with a graceful growth habit, small but interesting flowers, ornamental fruit, and brilliant, long-lasting fall foliage coloration.

Like many plants in the rose family, cotoneaster is susceptible to a variety of pests and diseases, but if it is sited correctly these problems tend to be less of a concern. Pruning should be kept to a minimum and is usually performed only if there is a need to remove dead or diseased branches or to reduce plant size. Cotoneasters thrive in full sun or partial shade but also tolerate dense shade. They prefer moist, well-drained soils but are adaptable to both acidic and alkaline soils. Once established, these tough plants will tolerate drought and heat very well.

Cotoneaster works well in groupings, mass plantings, and foundation plantings. The low-growing species are effective as facer or edging plants and along rock walls and embankments.

Listed below are a few commonly known and worthy species. There are also several important evergreen cotoneasters, which can be found in the evergreen section of this book.

Cotoneaster adpressus (creeping cotoneaster)

This low-mounding shrub will grow to 1–2 ft. in height and spread 4–6 ft. The attractive, small pink flowers open in late spring and early summer. During the summer months, the petite, dark green leaves provide a fine texture in the landscape. The foliage will turn tones of deep orange, red, and purple and the color will persist well into the autumn season. Probably the most attractive feature of this plant is the cranberry-like fruit ripening in late summer and early fall. The fruit will remain well after the leaves have fallen off. Hardy from Zones

4–7 but best in a protected location in colder climates.

'Little Gem' is a charming, low-growing variety with glossy, dark green leaves and cascading sprays of branches. This compact plant is suitable along rock walls and raised flowerbeds and can be mixed with compatible dwarf plants.

Cotoneaster horizontalis (rockspray cotoneaster)

Like the creeping cotoneaster, rockspray is another low-growing species. As the name *C. horizontalis* suggests, rockspray cotoneaster offers a graceful, horizontally branched growth habit reaching 3 ft. in height and sprawling 6–8 ft. wide. One special attribute of this groundcover shrub is that it can easily be trained up walls and fences, taking on the appearance of a vine or tall shrub. The small, pink flowers, while not overwhelming, do offer aesthetic value and in the fall

Cascading branches of *C. horizontalis* 'Variegata'

transform into attractive bright red fruit. Each autumn gardeners can rely on an impressive display of fall foliage colors of red, orange, and maroon lasting late into the season.

Rockspray cotoneaster should be sited in full sun or partial shade where there is adequate moisture. Because of their graceful growth habit, pruning should be kept to a minimum. Any dead or damaged branches can be removed in early spring before the start of the growing season.

Rockspray cotoneaster is an outstanding plant for dramatic landscape effect. It is very effective in mass plantings, along walls, and in raised planters. Hardy from Zones 5–7.

'Variegata' has delicate leaves edged with white, which change to striking shades of red in fall. This is variety is slow growing and should be sited where more aggressive plants will not overwhelm it.

{ *Cytisus* spp.
Broom
Cytisus scoparius (Scotch broom)

This wispy, upright grower is native to Europe and has adapted well to American climates. The dark green, slender branches offer a finely textured broom-like look all year. Scotch broom's best attribute is the profusion of bright yellow flowers in spring. Broom is in the pea family and has very unusual, oddly shaped flowers and small, peapod-like fruit. In flower, this plant radiates with color for several weeks. Once flowering is finished, a small, green, three-part (trifoliate) leaf remains until fall.

Scotch broom is a fast growing shrub with an upright, often erratic growth habit and a shallow root system. Therefore, regular selective pruning in early spring will encourage a dense habit, decreasing the chances of top-heavy plants flopping over from weight. Some hand pruning can also be done after the plant has finished flowering in mid-spring.

This plant will adapt to a wide variety of soils and soil pH ranges and is most content in drier, well-drained soils and full sun. Scotch broom tolerates hot, dry conditions and will often be found thriving near the seashore, along highways, and on embankments. Although Scotch broom is a suitable plant for poor, infertile soils and hot, dry locations, it will also thrive in rich, well-drained garden soils.

It is excellent in mass plantings or as a companion plant to perennials or other flowering shrubs. Scotch broom is not a particularly long-lived plant and should be considered a short-term visitor in the garden. In most cases, brooms will look good for five to ten years in the garden, but usually only with regular and proper pruning. With optimum conditions and proper care, their usefulness can be significantly extended. Vigorous, healthy plants will produce copious amounts of blooms that will brighten up the garden in spring. Many gardeners feel the spectacular display of color in the spring is well worth Scotch broom's short-term presence in the garden. Hardy from Zones 5–8.

NOTABLE VARIETIES

'Lena'. Prominent ruby red flowers and somewhat compact growth habit.

'Lilac Time'. Lilac pink flowers offer nice tones of pink.

'Luna'. Bright yellow flowers shine in the landscape.

'Moonlight'. A very attractive form with creamy, luminous white flowers.

'Nova Scotia'. A very hardy form with yellow flowers.

'Zeelandia'. Pink, lilac, and red flowers provide a complementing contrast.

Cytisus x praecox (Warminster broom)

There are several popular varieties of Warminster broom (*Cytisus* x *praecox*), a common hybrid broom. This species is similar to Scotch broom in habit and ornamental qualities. It is highly cultivated and adapted to the United States' varying climates. Hardy from Zones 6–8. 'Allgold' has bright yellow flowers that provide a great show in spring. 'Hollandia' has salmon pink flowers, offering an unusual, rich color.

Daphne spp.
Daphne

Daphnes are very charming garden plants, well known for their incredibly fragrant flowers and attractive foliage. The dainty but colorful and sweetly fragrant flowers are unmatched by most flowering shrub species. Daphnes do have the reputation as somewhat finicky garden inhabitants, but there are several species and varieties that are suitable for the home garden. Daphnes are prized for their dwarf habit and ability to provide interest throughout most of the year. They work well in combination with other plants and can be the star of any home garden.

The key to successfully growing daphnes is to properly site the plants in an area of the garden with very specific environmental conditions. Daphnes must have very well-drained soil to flourish. They also prefer organic, rich soil with adequate and even moisture. In general, partial shade is best to protect daphne from the full exposure to sun and the elements, although some species will prosper in full sun if provided adequate moisture. Established plants do benefit from moderate but regular fertilization once or twice a year. In addition, 1–2 in. of mulch (such as crushed leaves, wood chips, or pine straw) will help to keep the roots cool during hot summer months. Daphnes should be watered during periods of drought and sheltered from windy locations. Some pruning is needed since older daphnes tend to be susceptible to breakage from heavy snow loads and weak branching unions. Modest pruning after flowering will help to maintain dense growth habit and reduce branch damage.

Daphne x burkwoodii (Burkwood daphne)

This hybrid daphne has a dense growth habit, reaching 3–4 ft. tall with a similar spread. Pink flower buds arranged in rounded clusters open to white flowers in mid-spring and will provide an attractive display for several weeks. This sweetly fragrant shrub is an excellent choice for the home garden.

Burkwood daphne should be given moist, organic, well-drained soil and partial or filtered sunlight. Occasional pruning to remove old or weak stems will help to keep plants dense and productive.

The variegated foliage of 'Carol Mackie' daphne

'Jim's Pride' daphne in flower

© John Bieber

'Carol Mackie' is a popular variegated form with creamy yellow leaf edges. It is excellent as an accent plant or in grouping combined with other low-growing garden plants. Best from Zones 4–7.

Daphne x transatlantica (hybrid daphne)

This flowering shrub has often been confused with the Caucasian daphne (*Daphne caucasica*) in commerce, but the two are separate species. This upright shrub offers fragrant, white, star-shaped flowers starting in mid spring and continuing sporadically through the summer and fall. The sweet aroma from the flowers is intoxicating and will quickly win over even the pickiest gardener. The smooth, green leaves offer a soft texture during the summer and into the fall. This hybrid daphne will grow 4–5 ft. tall with a similar spread.

As with all daphnes, regular pruning to keep plants dense and vigorous will provide long-term benefits.

Full sun or partial shade is acceptable but dense shade should be avoided. If sited correctly, it is one of the hardiest and adaptable daphnes available.

This hybrid daphne is a reliable performer suitable in groupings, woodland gardens, rock gardens, and shrub borders mixed with perennials. It performs well in Zones 5–7, but it will also grow in Zones 4 and 8 with special siting and additional care.

'Jim's Pride' was named for Jim Cross, founder of Environmentals Nursery on Long Island, New York. It was named by the newly formed Daphne Society.

Daphne odora (winter daphne)

This beautiful evergreen species is native to China. It is called winter daphne because of its ability to flower in mid to late winter and early spring. The interesting purple flower buds open to pinkish white flowers. This shrub is a reliable performer in warmer climates and can also be grown in containers and brought indoors in northern climates. However, the variety 'Aureomarginata' is hardier than the species and will grow outdoors in many areas of the northeastern United States. The dark, glossy green leaves offer a rich, bold texture in the landscape. Winter daphne will grow 3–4 ft. or more tall with an equal spread.

Winter daphne is a tough, adaptable landscape plant that will thrive in moist, well-drained soil and partial shade. This winter-blooming shrub can effectively be used in groupings, rock gardens, woodland gardens, foundation plantings, and is especially useful in containers. It offers a wonderful, unique fragrance when most plants are dormant. Hardy from Zones 7–9.

'Aureomarginata' is a striking variegated form with yellow leaf edges. Hardier than the species, it will survive the northern limits of Zone 7 and possibly Zone 6 with protection.

Foliage and flower of *D. odora* 'Aureomarginata'

Deutzia spp.
Deutzia

Deutzia is a well-known, old-fashioned flowering shrub admired for its ability to produce a profusion of showy spring flowers. Flowers range from white to deep pink, single or double, depending on the variety. In spring, cascading branches will be covered with a dense display of colorful flowers. Deutzia has a strong, upright or spreading growth habit and medium green foliage. These graceful shrubs range in size from 4–8 ft. tall. Fall foliage coloration is usually not overwhelming, with the exception of slender deutzia (*Deutzia gracilis*), with leaves often tinged with purple. In general, deutzia is most evident in spring, when it displays its masses of showy flowers. After flowering, deutzia also exhibits a graceful habit and lush, medium green leaves.

Deutzia is an easy plant to grow and will adapt to most soils, light exposures, and landscape situations. Deutzia blooms on previous year's growth, so maintenance pruning should be done right after flowering to keep the plant dense and productive. If plants are in poor health, severe nonselective pruning may be needed. In this situation, shrubs can be pruned to 6 in. from the ground, which will result in a flush of new, vigorous vegetative growth the first season followed by flowers the second season.

In general, deutzia is very effective as a mass planting, small grouping, shrub border, background plant, and foundation plant.

There are several deutzia species and hybrids, many of which possess valuable garden merit. The list of varieties below describes some of the best and most popular selections available. These selections provide impressive aesthetic value and function in the landscape. Hardy from Zones 5–8.

NOTABLE VARIETIES

D. × 'Magician'. Beautiful deep pink flowers with a white stripe along the edge of the petals give the individual flowers a two-tone coloration. Excellent as a background plant or in groupings and effectively used as a backdrop in perennial borders.

D. × Pink-A-Boo ('Monzia'). A beautifully graceful grower with arching branches and waves of pink flowers.

D. scabra 'Flore-pleno'. Also known as 'Plena', this attractive variety offers white, double flowers with an unusual ruffled look. This plant can reach 6–8 ft. in height and should be used as a background plant or in groupings.

Mounded growth habit of *D. gracilis* 'Nikko' in flower

D. scabra 'Pink Minor'. A fairly compact variety to 3 ft. tall with an equal spread. Attractive light pink flowers and dense growth habit make this variety ideal in foundation plantings and in mixed plant borders.

D. scabra 'Pride of Rochester'. Light pink, double flowers provide a nice show of soft pastel color.

D. × 'Rosalind'. This graceful shrub has an upright growth habit to 5 ft. tall and deep pink flowers.

Deutzia gracilis (slender deutzia)

Slender deutzia has a distinct mounded growth habit to 3 ft. in height with a spread of 3–4 ft. The attractive white flowers are borne on upright spikes in midspring, providing a great splash of midseason color. The small, deep green, pointed leaves are typically tinged with shades of purple in the autumn.

Like many other deutzias, slender deutzia is easy to grow and adapts well to almost any landscape situation. Slender deutzia thrives in well,-drained, moist

Deep pink flowers of *Deutzia* 'Magician'

soils and full sun but is remarkably tolerant of poor soils and shade. Pruning with a hand shear right after flowering will maintain a dense, neat grower. If neglected, these shrubs may appear sparse or leggy, and an early spring pruning to 6 in. will quickly rejuvenate the plant. Slender deutzia has no major pest problems and is exceptionally drought tolerant and cold hardy. This native to Japan has acclimated well to the varying climates of the United States.

Because it has a spreading, graceful growth habit, slender deutzia is suitable as an edging plant, shrub border, mixed with perennials, and in foundation plantings. Hardy from Zones 4–8.

'Nikko' is one of the best low-growing shrubs available, reaching only 2 ft. high with double the spread. This groundcover-like shrub will have white flower clusters in spring and striking deep maroon foliage that will be the highlight of the fall garden year after year. A perfect complement to the home garden with limited room.

Diervilla sessilifolia
Southern bush honeysuckle

This low-growing, spreading shrub has rich, glossy green foliage and unusual, interesting, yellow, tubular flowers in summer. The new foliage emerges coppery purple before maturing to dark green. In addition, leaves will often be tinged with purple in the autumn. The flowers, while not overwhelming individually, are striking in clusters along the tips of the stems. The flowers present a nice display in mid to late summer. Although southern bush honeysuckle is not too aggressive, it will steadily creep along in the garden, creating a dense grouping of branches. Each plant will spread up to 5–6 ft. with a height of 3–5 ft.

Southern bush honeysuckle prefers moist, well-drained soil and full sun but also tolerates some shade. This plant is pest resistant and adaptable to many garden situations. Pruning can be kept to a minimum, although a hard pruning to 6 in. every few years will keep the plants compact and floriferous.

Because southern bush honeysuckle has a low, spreading habit, it is appropriate in mass plantings, along embankments, or as an edging plant. It is even effective in containers or when combined with perennials in a flower border. Southern bush honeysuckle is native to the southeastern United States and is hardy from Zones 4–7.

'Butterfly' has intense yellow flowers and attractive purple fall foliage color.

Enkianthus spp.
Enkianthus

Enkianthus is an interesting flowering shrub and is closely related to rhododendrons and azaleas. The beautiful small, bell- or urn-shaped flowers can vary in color from pure white to deep pink in mid to late spring, depending on the species or variety. The small, dark green leaves will change to glorious shades of yellow, orange, red, and maroon in the fall. Like a fine wine, enkianthus gets better with age. As the plant matures, the layered growth habit and smooth brown-gray bark become more evident, particularly in the winter.

Enkianthus likes moist, organic, acidic, well-drained soil. The use of mulch or compost is very beneficial to these garden treasures since they have very fine, delicate root systems. Enkianthus will grow in full sun or partial shade but is best in light shade, especially in warmer climates. Pruning should be kept to a minimum and is usually only done to remove dead or rubbing branches. Enkianthus has no serious pest problems and is a reliable performer, provided it receives the cultural requirements it needs.

Enkianthus is grown as a medium to large shrub, depending on the species or variety you choose. It is ideal in woodland gardens mixed with plants—such as rhododendrons, azaleas, and dogwoods—requiring the same cultural needs.

Enkianthus campanulatus (redvein enkianthus)

This species usually grows as a large shrub to 8 ft. tall but can grow over 15 ft. tall in ideal conditions. The creamy, pale yellow, bell-shaped flowers are accented with distinct red veins in great profusion for several weeks in the spring. The shades of deep orange, bright red, and purple fall foliage color will grab your attention along the garden path. Gardeners must be patient with this plant, as it takes a few years to establish and has a modest growth rate. Undoubtedly, redvein enkianthus is an elegant shrub that will improve as it matures and is well worth the wait. Hardy from Zones 4–7. This shrub should be sited in a protected location in Zone 4.

'Red Bells' is a more compact variety than the species and has beautiful flowers streaked with deep red veins, giving the flowers a red coloration.

Enkianthus perulatus (white enkianthus)

White enkianthus is quite an unusual, hard-to-find shrub that is considered by many gardeners one of the most beautiful plants for fall foliage color. This compact, slow grower will reach 5–6 ft. in height and equal spread over thirty years. Established plants develop a very artistic, mounded growth habit over time. The small, white, urn-shaped flowers occur in mass along each stem in spring. Even though the dangling flowers are quite attractive, the most admirable attribute of white enkianthus is the small, dark green leaves that change to deep scarlet red in the fall, persisting for several weeks. The variation in red tones of the foliage is stunning.

White enkianthus prefers well-drained, moist, and acidic soils. For best fall coloration, plants should be grown in full sun or partial shade. Pruning should be kept to a minimum and is only recommended to remove dead branches or damaged stems.

White enkianthus in flower

It is highly coveted by plant collectors and garden enthusiasts alike. This unique shrub is suitable in the home garden where space is limited. It also works nicely with rhododendrons, azaleas, dogwoods, hollies, and other acidic-soil-loving plants in dappled shade. Since white enkianthus is a slow-growing shrub, it is important to site it correctly in areas of the garden where it will not be out-competed by other plants. Although it is slow to establish, taking years to reach any reasonable size, it is well worth the wait. This native to Japan is well adapted to the climate on the East Coast of the United States. Hardy from Zones 5–7.

'Compacta' is an extremely slow growing selection, reaching only 18 in. tall. Excellent for rock gardens, dwarf conifer gardens, or in combination with other compact growers.

Red fall foliage color of white enkianthus

{ *Forsythia* spp.
Forsythia

Forsythia is one of the most well-known and recognizable flowering shrubs in gardens today. It was named in honor of William Forsyth (1737–1804), a distinguished Scottish horticulturist. Forsythia is easily identified by the flush of golden yellow flowers in early spring. To many gardeners, blooming forsythia signifies the unofficial start of spring. After the flowers finish, medium to dark green leaves emerge, providing lush vegetation all summer. The fall foliage color is variable and can change from yellow to shades of reddish purple. The beautiful, arching branches cascade down to the ground in a very graceful manner that is equally attractive in the winter months.

Forsythia is a very adaptable shrub and will tolerate varying types of soils, light exposures, and even pollution. Full sun and well-drained, moist soil provides optimum conditions for this plant to thrive. Forsythia is also very tolerant of pruning and unfortunately is often incorrectly pruned by unsuspecting homeowners. These resilient shrubs are frequently pruned into unnatural rounded shapes or box-shaped formal hedges. This tight shearing process reduces flowering potential and ruins the natural, arching growth habit of forsythia. To maximize their beauty, plants should be allowed to grow naturally in mass plantings or as informal hedges and screens. Removing older stems every few years will promote new, healthy branches from the base of the plant. An occasional severe, rejuvenation pruning in late winter or early spring will also renovate unproductive shrubs. Since forsythia blooms on previous year's growth, flowers will be sacrificed for one year. However, gardeners will be pleasantly surprised by an impressive display of color in the second season.

Although there are many large-growing types of forsythias available, a few are suitable for the home landscape. Forsythia can be used in groupings, mass plantings, background plantings, or as informal hedges. They can possess great function in the landscape if the time is taken to site them correctly. Forsythia branches can also be cut and brought indoors in late winter and forced into flower.

Border forsythia in a mass planting

Forsythia x intermedia (border forsythia)

Border forsythia is a large, spreading shrub growing 8 ft. tall and 12 ft. wide. It is a fast-growing plant that will flower heavily even at an early age. It should be sited in full sun or partial shade and given plenty of room.

Although border forsythia can overwhelm a small garden with its robust size, regular selective pruning to remove older stems will keep plants in scale, reducing the possibility of overgrown plantings. Shrubs can also be lightly pruned after flowering to reduce the size. Border forsythia is very effective in a home garden as an informal hedge, mass planting, and as a barrier plant or screen. Border forsythia will successfully camouflage an old shed or block a view to a neighboring house. Best from Zones 6–8, but it may also grow from Zones 5 and 9 if sited correctly.

Border forsythia flowers

NOTABLE VARIETIES

'Beatrix Ferrand'. This handsome variety offers large, golden yellow flowers in early spring. Named after the famous American garden designer.

'Fiesta'. This variegated cultivar has interesting combinations of green and yellow in its leaves. This plant also has interesting red stems and works well as an accent in the landscape.

Gold Tide ('Courtasol'). A compact, low-growing variety with medium green leaves and profuse clusters of yellow flowers. It is an excellent plant as a ground-cover or in mass plantings.

'Lynwood'. This selection provides a brilliant display of yellow flowers and an upright growth habit. One of the most reliable varieties available, it originated in Ireland.

'Spring Glory'. An early flowering type with bright yellow flowers.

Forsythia viridissima (green-stem forsythia)

This unusual species is not particularly popular, but the variety 'Bronxensis' is gaining popularity in local nurseries. 'Bronxensis' is suitable for the home landscape since it is truly a dwarf, only growing to 1 ft. tall. It will spread 2–3 ft. and creep along the ground as it grows. The attractive yellow flowers in spring are followed by medium green leaves in summer. The flowers are usually not as showy as the large forsythia types. The bright green stems are attractive during the winter months.

This low, mounded shrub will tolerate various types of soils and light exposures but prefers well-drained soil and full sun. Unproductive plants can be pruned to the ground and easily rejuvenated. Because green-stem forsythia essentially grows as a groundcover, it is very useful as an edging plant, in groupings, rock gardens, and foundation plantings. Hardy from Zones 5–8.

'Arnold Dwarf' is another well-known dwarf variety that also offers a compact, mounded habit. It will grow 3 ft. tall and spread twice as wide. 'Arnold Dwarf' is suitable in mass plantings, as an edging plant, and is functional in a foundation planting. Eager gardeners should be patient since new plants usually need a few years to establish before the pale yellow flowers will develop in profusion. Hardy from Zones 5–8.

Fothergilla gardenii
Dwarf fothergilla

Dwarf fothergilla is a handsome shrub native to the southeastern United States. It is a member of the witch hazel family (Hamamelidaceae), which has the admirable reputation of exhibiting unusual flowers and exquisite fall color. This multistemmed, upright shrub has white, fragrant, bottlebrush-like flower spikes in spring. The unusual, fuzzy, fragrant flowers will last for several weeks and are followed by rounded, dark green, textured leaves. The leaves turn brilliant shades of yellow, orange, red, and maroon in autumn, and the fall foliage is arguably the best attribute of this lovely shrub. Plants grow to 3–5 ft. tall with a similar spread and form a dense habit.

Although fothergilla is quite tolerant of sandy and heavy clay soils, they will thrive in moist, well-drained,

Fothergilla with brilliant fall color

© Vincent A. Simeone

not quite as brilliant as other varieties but still worth consideration because of the excellent spring and summer interest.

'Mt. Airy'. One of the best selections for fall foliage color. The rich, dark green summer foliage changes to extraordinary combinations of orange, red, and purple in fall. This variety also produces abundant, showy white flowers in spring. 'Mt Airy' is a vigorous grower, reaching 5–6 ft. in height with a similar spread. It was selected by Dr. Michael Dirr from the University of Georgia.

acidic soils. Fothergilla will flower best in full sun, but partial shade is also acceptable. Fothergilla is a trouble-free shrub with no major pest problems, making it a pleasurable plant to grow. Fothergilla seldom needs pruning, but occasional selective pruning to remove old, unproductive branches may be beneficial. In addition, leggy, sparse shrubs can be lightly pruned after flowering to promote a compact, dense growth habit.

Dwarf Fothergilla is an excellent shrub for mass plantings, small groupings, woodland gardens, foundation plantings, and is also effective in perennial borders. This beautiful, user-friendly shrub provides landscape interest in spring, summer, and fall. Hardy from Zones 5–8 but may grow in Zones 4 and 9 with special siting.

NOTABLE VARIETIES

'Blue Mist'. This truly dwarf plant has unusual leaves tinged with a waxy blue color. The fall foliage color is

'Mt Airy' fothergilla in flower

{ *Hamamelis* spp.
Witch hazel

The witch hazel family (Hamamelidaceae) contains some of the most beautiful and unusual flowering shrubs and trees in the world. Although the common witch hazel native to North America blooms in the autumn, the winter-blooming Asian species and hybrids are the most popular and sought after for the garden. Witch hazels are best known for their curly, straplike flowers in late winter. These extraordinary flowers will burst open like party

'Arnold Promise' witch hazel blooming in the landscape

streamers and glow in the winter sun. On extremely cold days the flowers will close up to avoid damage from freezing temperatures. Certain species and varieties will provide a moderate fragrance, and cut branches can be easily forced into bloom indoors. Witch hazel also has a wide spreading, vase-shaped growth habit and dark green, textured leaves that change to golden yellow, orange, and occasionally red in the fall.

Witch hazels prefer moist, well-drained soil with plenty of organic matter. Pruning should be kept to a minimum since over-pruning will ruin their interesting, graceful growth habit.

Hamamelis is one of a few select shrub genera that flowers in the winter. For this reason, witch hazels should be used as specimen plants, in groupings, and in close proximately to a window or view from the house. However, the witch hazels listed in this section are all wide-spreading, large shrubs with the potential to reach 10–15 ft. wide with an equal height. Although they are medium to slow growing, witch hazels can quickly outgrow the space that has been allocated to them in the garden. When choosing a witch hazel for the garden, remember to site the plant where it will have plenty of room to grow. The three species described below are hardy from Zones 5–8.

Hamamelis mollis (Chinese witch hazel)

Chinese witch hazel has fragrant, bright yellow, straplike flowers with red centers in winter. The fuzzy, dark green leaves emerge in spring and turn brilliant shades of yellow and orange in fall. The picturesque, layered, and spreading growth habit is prominent during the winter months when the plant is leafless.

Hamamelis × intermedia (hybrid witch hazel)

This hybrid witch hazel is the most popular and commercially available of the group. This vigorous grower displays an upright, vase-shaped growth habit that will spread as it matures. Flowers range in color from bright yellow to orange and red in late winter. The fall foliage color is also variable and can range from yellow to orange and deep red.

This species is easy to grow and is typically quicker to establish then other types of witch hazel. It is adaptable to various types of soils but is best in moist, well-drained soil and full sun or partial shade.

NOTABLE VARIETIES

'Arnold Promise'. A very popular variety with large, bright yellow flowers with red centers and showy fall color. Excellent in groupings or as a single specimen.

'Diane'. This form has striking brick red flowers, making it very prominent in the winter landscape, especially against a snowy background. This variety is truly spectacular when in full flower.

'Jelena'. This is one of my favorite selections, with large, bright coppery orange flowers and attractive orange-red fall foliage color.

'Primavera'. Bright yellow flowers are accented with rich red centers.

'Ruby Glow'. The deep coppery red flowers provide a robust color in the landscape.

From right to left: Flowers of 'Jelena', 'Arnold Promise', and 'Diane'

{ Heptacodium miconioides
Seven-son flower

This tall, upright shrub has many pleasing attributes to offer the home garden. This unique flowering shrub offers a very distinct appearance unlike any shrub in the landscape. The dark green, bold leaves have pronounced veins and a wonderful texture. The small, creamy white flowers appear in late summer, followed by clusters of deep red calyces, which are the appendages that surround the flower. This aesthetically pleasing effect is quite striking and long lasting. The smooth, flaking bark provides interest all year and is highlighted during the winter months.

Seven-son flower is an adaptable plant that thrives in moist, organic soil but will tolerate poor, sandy soils. It prefers full sun or partial shade and responds well to pruning. Special selective pruning to train plants as

Heptacodium in fall

H. syriacus 'Diana' in a mass planting

small trees and expose the beautiful bark is a worthwhile goal. Individual specimens can reach 15 ft. high or more and slightly less in spread.

This wonderful native to China is excellent as a small specimen tree, in mass plantings, or small groupings. Seven-son flower provides great texture in the garden and works well as a backdrop to smaller plants. It is primarily considered a shrub for mid- to late-summer interest but can offer year-round interest as well. Hardy from Zones 5–8.

{ *Hibiscus syriacus*
Rose of Sharon

Many of us have fond childhood memories of rose of Sharon shrubs growing in our garden along with other colorful garden favorites such as poppies, peonies, and azaleas. The showy white, pink, or red flowers—resembling the tropical hibiscus flowers that grow in warmer climates of the world—emerge

'Blue Bird' rose of Sharon flower

in mid to late summer and sporadically continue through the fall. These shrubs have a stout, upright growth habit reaching 8–10 ft. tall with half the spread.

Rose of Sharon is fast growing and will respond well to pruning in early spring, which will stimulate an abundance of summer flowers. This reliable summer bloomer prefers well-drained, moist soil but will also tolerate poor soils. For best performance, plants should be sited in full sun but will also do reasonably well in partially shaded areas of the garden. While this flowering shrub is prone to several pest problems, these problems do not seem to discourage it from flowering consistently every year.

Rose of Sharon combines well with herbaceous plants in perennial borders and can be useful as a screen, informal hedge, and in groupings. It can also be used as a single specimen in a lawn. Rose of Sharon will catch the eye in the heat of summer. Hardy from Zones 5–8, possibly Zone 9 with additional care.

NOTABLE VARIETIES

'Blue Bird'. An unusual selection offering violet blue flowers with dark red centers.

'Diana'. A prolific bloomer with large, pure white flowers that will brighten up the landscape.

Assorted Hydrangea varieties

{ *Hydrangea* spp.
Hydrangea

Hydrangeas are among the most diverse and widely used shrubs in the world, with dozens of species and hundreds of varieties used in private and public gardens, large and small. The voluptuous flowers of hydrangea are available in a wide range of colors, shapes, and sizes, from large globes to delicate lacey types. Some of the most beautiful and unique varieties can be found in Europe, where they have been an integral part of gardening for centuries. Our fascination with hydrangeas is the result of the great admiration for their rich colors that paint our landscape. These dependable performers will flower in mid to late summer and frequently into the fall. Once the cold weather arrives, hydrangeas will continue to display floral interest as the faded flowers dry on the plant and persist into winter.

But besides the awesome display of color during the summer and fall seasons, hydrangeas provide other important attributes. Hydrangeas offer a wide range of rich foliage textures and, in some cases, excellent multicolored fall foliage. They also develop into many different sizes from dwarf, 2 ft. by 2 ft. plants to large shrubs reaching 12 ft. or more in height. Whichever hydrangeas you choose, you will not be disappointed with their reliable, long-lasting beauty.

The care and cultivation of hydrangeas is somewhat specific, and special attention should be given to these shrubs to maximize their potential. Hydrangeas in general prefer moist, well-drained soils, and several species are quite drought and heat sensitive. Even a well-watered hydrangea will wilt in the extreme heat of the unrelenting summer sun. The fleshy, new growth requires ample moisture to keep plants turgid. Therefore, hydrangeas should be sited specifically in the landscape to ensure they will prosper. Partial shade is ideal in warmer climates to protect them from the scorching summer sun. In northern states, hydrangeas can be sited in full sun, but adequate watering is important. Soil pH—the acidity or alkalinity of the soil—will affect the color of the flowers in some species and varieties, such as bigleaf hydrangea (*Hydrangea macrophylla*). Rich, organic, fertile soils are best, but hydrangeas will tolerate variations in these soil specifications.

Proper pruning techniques are essential for the care and cultivation of these popular flowering shrubs. Pruning of hydrangeas is quite complex, since each hydrangea species has a different requirement. Careful research must be done to make certain that the proper pruning techniques are being applied. For example, hydrangeas either bloom on current season's growth or previous season's growth, depending on the species or variety chosen. Because of this, different pruning techniques are performed to maximize flower production and encourage vigorous growth. Detailed requirements are addressed under each species below.

Hydrangeas can be used in numerous landscape situations such as small groupings, mass plantings, and in foundation plantings. They are also very effective when used in shade gardens or as companions to herbaceous perennials. In addition, hydrangea flowers make great cut flowers in an arrangement and can be used fresh or dried.

Hydrangea hardiness varies, and careful selection and situating in the garden is essential, especially in colder climates.

Hydrangea arborescens (smooth hydrangea)

This floriferous shrub gets its name from the smooth stems and leaves. The white, pom-pom-like flowers provide a wave of color in summer. The rounded flowers begin as small, greenish balls and develop into large, globular flowers reaching 6 in. in diameter. The wide, lush foliage adds a wonderful coarse texture in the landscape. The slender stems develop into clumps of mounded, open growth.

The smooth hydrangea will flower on the current season's growth; therefore, shrubs should be cut to 6 in. from the ground in late winter or early spring to promote vigorous regrowth and good flower production during the growing season. Like most hydrangea species, *H. arborescens* prefers full sun or partial shade and well-drained, moist soils. This is a very hardy hydrangea, growing in Zones 3–9. Shrubs in Zone 3 will likely need to be protected from harsh winter temperatures. Because smooth hydrangea flowers on the current season's growth, even if stems are killed to the ground due to severe cold, they will likely still flower provided the roots have not been damaged.

This American native grows 3–5 ft. tall with a similar spread and is very effective in mass plantings, shrub borders, shade gardens, and foundation plantings. The cut flowers are also very useful and will last a long time in dried flower arrangements.

NOTABLE VARIETIES

'Annabelle'. Extremely large, white flowers reaching 8 in. in diameter or more. Very beautiful show of color in summer and also very effective as a cut flower.

'Grandiflora'. This well-known variety is called the hills of snow hydrangea because of its large, showy white flowers that look like puffs of snow in summer. This is a very common variety and a reliable performer.

Hydrangea macrophylla
(bigleaf hydrangea, florist hydrangea)

This species is easily the most common garden hydrangea available in commerce. It is a beloved garden favorite by professionals and novice gardeners alike because of its numerous and delightful attributes. Bigleaf hydrangea is an aesthetically pleasing, easy-to-grow shrub that will dazzle the home garden with bright colors and bold textures.

The large, showy flowers arrive just in time to complement the glorious colors of the midsummer garden. Flowers range in color from white to pink, purple, and blue, depending on the variety and growing conditions. The actual flower consists of many florets, which look like mini flowers. There are two

Mophead hydrangea flowers

Lacecap hydrangea in flower

distinct types of flowers, mopheads and lacecaps, which are quite different. Mopheads, also called "hortensias," are the typical large, round hydrangea flowers that are found in the landscape and floral industry. Lacecaps are flat-topped flowers with a combination of showy florets along the outer rim and less conspicuous fertile flowers in the center. These two distinctly different flower parts within the same flower head provide an interesting contrast. Over the past ten years, lacecap hydrangeas have become very popular garden plants.

In addition to its flowers, bigleaf hydrangea exhibits large, round fleshy leaves and an upright, dense growth habit. Well-established plants can grow into 3–6 ft. mounds if properly sited. Leaves usually do not offer any vibrant colors in fall and often change to a muted yellow.

Since its foliage is very fleshy, bigleaf hydrangea can be susceptible to drought and heat stress. For this reason, partial shade exposure is recommended, although plants will also grow in full sun provided they have adequate moisture. While it is generally true that hydrangeas like moist conditions, these plants have been known to grow near the seashore and will adapt to many landscape situations. During the heat of the summer, hydrangeas benefit from deep watering with an irrigation system or individual garden sprinkler. However, bigleaf hydrangeas like well-drained soil, and shrubs located in poorly drained soils will not perform as well.

One very important environmental condition that affects flower color of this species is soil pH. A soil pH of 7.0 is recognized as neutral, with anything less than 7.0 considered acidic while anything higher than 7.0 is considered alkaline. In acidic soils, hydrangea flowers turn shades of blue or purple. In alkaline, or "sweet," soils, flowers will turn pink. However, with some of the improved varieties pH is less of a factor. To manipulate

soil pH, several methods can be used. The addition of aluminum sulfate or iron sulfate products will lower soil pH, while the addition of lime or calcium products will raise soil pH. This must be done gradually because too much of these products may cause plant damage. Visit your local garden center, nursery, or local extension office for more information on proper applications of these products.

Pruning bigleaf hydrangea can be a challenging task, and is very dependent on the health and intended function of the plant. Since bigleaf hydrangea flowers on the previous season's wood, shrubs should not be severely pruned on a regular basis—flowers will be compromised the following year. To keep your shrubs healthy and productive, one of two methods can be used. Hydrangeas can be selectively pruned in early spring, which will reduce the amount of blooms the first year but will invigorate the plant. The goal is to selectively remove weaker stems, both old and new, leaving only the strongest stems to develop. Or plants can be lightly pruned right after flowering to reduce size or to reshape the plant. This will help to maintain a dense and well-groomed shrub. Avoid pruning in the fall since flower buds may not have a chance to develop properly. Such late pruning will result in less flower production. If pruning is done correctly, shrubs will set flower buds for the flowing year.

A more drastic measure of pruning on non-productive plants is to drastically prune the entire plant down to the ground in late winter or early spring. Flowers will be sacrificed for one season, but the lush new growth will yield flowers the second year. Occasionally in cold climates, unusually cold temperatures will frequently kill the top growth of hydrangeas, resulting in strong vegetative growth during the growing season but no flowers. Gardeners will have to be patient and wait until next year to enjoy the beautiful flowers.

Bigleaf hydrangea is a corsely textured shrub displaying vivid colors. It can be used in mass plantings, small groupings, foundation plantings, mixed perennial borders, and as a small specimen. It is an excellent companion plant to many herbaceous perennials. This species is also heavily used in the floral industry as a cut flower or spring holiday plant.

Bigleaf hydrangea is hardy from Zones 6–9, but a few select varieties will grow in Zones 4 and 5 if sited correctly.

NOTABLE VARIETIES

While there are many excellent varieties, here are a few worthwhile favorites for the home garden.

'Blue Wave' in flower

'Ayesha'. A very interesting form with cup-shaped florets and deep green, glossy leaves. The foliage is outstanding and will provide a wonderful backdrop to other garden plants. Flower color is dependent on soil pH.

'Blue Wave'. A dense, upright shrub with beautiful, rich blue lacecap flowers in acidic soils.

'Dooley'. A very vigorous, fast-growing variety with large, blue flowers in midsummer. It is a unique hydrangea since flowers occur on lateral branches of both new and older growth.

Endless Summer ('Bailmer'). A beautiful variety with large, round blooms up to 8 in. in diameter. In acidic soils flowers are a bright blue, and in alkaline soils they are pink. Unlike most bigleaf hydrangea varieties, Endless Summer blooms on the current season's growth and is a repeat bloomer. The endless crop of beautiful flowers will continue most of the summer and into the autumn. It is also one of the hardiest varieties, surviving the cold temperatures of Zone 4, but it will also thrive in warmer climates.

'Glowing Embers'. Large, deep rose-colored flowers and an upright growth habit to 6 ft.

'Madame Emile Mouillere'. A striking selection with pure white, globular flowers.

'Nikko Blue'. A mounded, dense plant with large, deep blue flowers in acidic soils. This is a common variety and reliable grower. 'Nikko Blue' is very effective in mass plantings, displaying an impressive show of color and texture.

'Pia'. A very charming dwarf variety with deep pink flowers and glossy green leaves. Plants will grow 2–3

'Pia' has petite pink flowers

ft. wide and high. Excellent when mixed with other dwarf plants in landscapes with limited space.

'Variegata'. This lacecap hydrangea has beautiful variegated leaves with creamy white edges. It is an excellent accent plant with its attractive foliage, compact growth habit, and interesting flowers.

Hydrangea serrata

A closely related species, *Hydrangea serrata*, is typically smaller in stature than bigleaf hydrangea. The leaves, stems, and flowers tend to be smaller but equally as beautiful. In addition, this species is reliably hardier than bigleaf hydrangea, growing in Zones 5–7. This plant is very appropriate for the home garden and should be used more often.

NOTABLE VARIETIES

'Bluebird'. An attractive lacecap with beautiful blue flowers in acidic soils. 'Bluebird' is a very vigorous grower, to 5 ft. in height and spread.

'Preziosa'. A compact grower with gorgeous flowers marbled with various shades of pink.

Hydrangea paniculata (panicle hydrangea)

The panicle hydrangea is a large, upright shrub with panicles of rounded or pyramidal white flowers in late summer and early fall. The 6–8 in. long flowers are not affected by soil pH and will eventually change to pink or purple as they mature. The medium green leaves

Panicle hydrangea in the landscape

Panicle hydrangea flower in fall

spring to stimulate new growth in the growing season.

Because of its size, panicle hydrangea is suitable as a small specimen in a lawn and is also functional as an informal hedge, screen, or background plant in a shrub border. I have also seen this shrub used very effectively in decorative containers and urns. It is a very cold hardy species, growing from Zones 3–8.

NOTABLE VARIETIES
'Grandiflora'. This is a very old and common variety with large, white flowers to 12 in. long. Also known as the "Pee Gee" hydrangea.

'Pee Wee'. A semi-dwarf form with smaller flowers than most other varieties.

'Pink Diamond'. The interesting white flowers change to rich pink as the season progresses.

'Tardiva'. A late bloomer with showy, white pyramidal flowers lasting well into the fall season.

Hydrangea quercifolia (oakleaf hydrangea)
Oakleaf hydrangea is undoubtedly one of the most beautiful and functional hydrangeas for the home garden. The dark green, coarsely textured leaves resemble the leaves of an oak tree and turn deep crimson to purple in the fall. The white, pyramidal flowers emerge in early to midsummer and often change to pink as they mature. Oakleaf hydrangea exhibits a dense, mounded growth habit that ranges from 4–8 ft. in height and spread. Older plants will exhibit a beautiful cinnamon brown flaking bark on mature stems.

will sometimes display tinges of red or purple in the fall. This plant can vary in size but usually grows as a tall, upright shrub with graceful, arching branches. Plants can easily reach 10 ft. or more in height and are suitable as large shrubs or small single-stemmed trees.

Panicle hydrangea thrives in rich, moist, well-drained garden soils but is very adaptable to various soil types. Full sun or partial shade is preferable, and too much shade will reduce flower production. Panicle hydrangea blooms on the current season's growth, so it should be pruned in winter or early

The beautiful, textured foliage of oakleaf hydrangea

'Alice' oakleaf hydrangea in flower

Oakleaf hydrangea is a pleasure to grow and will provide years of enjoyment if cared for properly. This shrub is adaptable to many landscape situations but prefers moist, well-drained soil, full sun or partial shade. Oakleaf hydrangea is one of the more drought-tolerant and pest-resistant hydrangea species available. Pruning can be done after flowers fade in late summer. Do not prune too late into the season or you may reduce flowering the following year. To rejuvenate older shrubs, selective pruning in early spring is recommended.

This multifaceted shrub is very functional in a shrub border, mass planting, shade garden, and foundation planting. Because of its bold texture and size, the dwarf varieties listed are more suitable for the home garden with limited space. Hardy from Zones 5–9.

NOTABLE VARIETIES

'Alice'. A large-growing and vigorous form with white flowers reaching 12 in. or more in length. This plant needs room and should only be used if given adequate space to grow.

'Pee Wee'. A delightful little shrub with small, white flowers. Ideal for the home landscape.

'Sikes Dwarf'. Another compact selection with an upright, densely branched growth habit.

'Snow Queen'. A reliable performer growing to 6 ft. tall and wide. The large, white flowers and bronzy red fall foliage make this plant very desirable in the landscape.

'Snowflake'. A very unusual selection, with double

white flowers exhibiting a lacey appearance. The large, heavy flowers droop off each branch in a graceful, weeping fashion. The flowers will change to pink in the fall and are spectacular in dried flower arrangements.

Hypericum spp.
St. John's wort

St. John's wort is a well-known, summer-blooming shrub with showy, golden yellow flowers and beautiful, smooth foliage. These reliable plants make great garden companions to other dwarf flowering shrubs and herbaceous plants. The striking, round, yellow flowers sparkle in the summer sunlight.

As a group, St. John's wort thrives in full sun and moist, well-drained soil. Adding mulch around the plants will help to keep the roots cool during the heat of the summer. To successfully grow St. John's wort, gardeners must be aware of their specific requirements. In general, St. John's wort performs better in cooler, less humid climates. However, several species and varieties are quite adaptable to many areas of the United Sates.

St. John's wort is a multistemmed shrub that is effective in mass plantings and foundation plantings. While the plants listed below are strictly ornamental, they are closely related to the St. John's wort used for medicinal purposes.

Hypericum calycinum (Aaron's beard St. John's wort)

This low-growing, creeping plant has beautiful blue-green foliage and bright yellow flowers in summer and early fall. Plantings can reach 12–18 in. in height and form large patches of growth. The masses of 3 in. diameter yellow flowers will brighten up the summer garden.

Aaron's beard is quite a tough plant and will tolerate poor, sandy soils but thrives in moist, well-drained, loamy garden soils. Full sun or partial shade will yield the best flower production. Cutting the plant down to the ground in late winter or early spring while plants are dormant will encourage new growth and flowers in the spring.

Since this plant is essentially a groundcover, it should be used in mass plantings, woodland gardens, and in combination with low-growing perennials and annuals. As a native of southern Europe and Asia Minor, Aaron's beard is best suited for cooler, moderate climates. In the U.S., it performs best in Zones 5–8.

Hypericum frondosum (golden St. John's wort)

This upright, flowering shrub is gaining in popularity and is emerging as one of the best species for American gardens. The handsome, blue-green leaves provide interest all summer and into the fall season. The bright, golden yellow flowers have densely clustered centers and offer a colorful, pleasant display in the garden. Plants will reach 3–4 ft. in height and spread, and as plants mature stems and branches will exfoliate, providing winter interest.

Golden St. John's wort is a very adaptable plant and will tolerate poor, sandy soils and drought. Plants will thrive in well-drained, moist, loamy soils and full sun or partial shade. Pruning is not often necessary but can be done periodically to keep and plants dense and vigorous.

Hypericum 'Tricolor'

This flowering shrub is very effective in shrub borders, foundation plantings, groupings, and is an excellent companion to perennial plantings. It is native to the southern United States and hardy from Zones 5–8. It is truly one of the most handsome midsummer bloomers available.

'Sunburst' has showy bright yellow flowers that seem to burst with color against the smooth canvas of the blue-green foliage. This densely growing variety is an excellent performer in the landscape.

Hypericum 'Hidcote' ('Hidcote' St. John's wort)

One of the most popular St. John's worts available, 'Hidcote' is a taller variety, growing 3–5 ft. high. The golden yellow flowers emerge in late spring or early summer, but flowers sporadically through the fall. The dark green, smooth-textured leaves provide a nice backdrop to the showy flowers. Hardy from Zones 6–8 but will grow in Zone 5 with protection.

Hypericum x *moseranum* (Moser's St. John's wort)

This hybrid St. John's wort has arching branches and interesting golden yellow flowers from midsummer to fall. The smooth, blue-green foliage is also very handsome. 'Tricolor' is the most popular garden variety of this plant. It has beautiful, white and rosy pink variegated leaves that provide interest even when the shrub is not in flower.

'Tricolor' should be pruned down to the ground each spring to encourage a new flush of growth the upcoming growing season. 'Tricolor' is very often treated as a herbaceous perennial and is an excellent companion plant to annuals and perennials. The variegated leaves also make this plant useful as an accent plant. This selection is best in Zone 7, and I have witnessed it performing reasonably well in hot, humid conditions.

H. androsaenum 'Albury Purple'

Hypericum androsaemum (Tutsan)

The species is seen regularly in European gardens but often fails in American gardens because it does not flourish in heat and humidity. However, the unusual selection 'Albury Purple' seems to adapt well and is available in commerce. It provides large, smooth, deep maroon leaves and small, delicate, yellow summer flowers. The newly emerging leaves display outstanding purple color as they unfold. In late summer and fall, the red to dark purple fleshy fruit provide a nice display as well.

This bushy, upright plant can grow several feet tall with a similar spread. Although this plant is hardy from Zones 6–8, it seems to perform better in cooler climates with less heat and humidity. Plants should be cut back to the ground in early spring to encourage the best foliage coloration, flowering, and fruit production.

Tutsan is effective in groupings and is useful when planted with herbaceous plants. It is also functional as an edging plant. Cut branches from tutsan are an excellent addition to floral arrangements. And it is a useful plant for foliage and fruit interest.

{ *Itea virginica*
Virginia Sweetspire

Virginia sweetspire is a wonderful native to the United State's East Coast and Midwest. This durable flowering shrub is worthy of praise because of its many wonderful garden traits. Virginia sweetspire has long, dangling white flower clusters offering a slight fragrance in late spring and early summer. One of sweetspire's best attributes is the dark green, smooth,

© Vincent A. Simeone

Virginia sweetspire 'Henry's Garnet' in the landscape

glossy leaves that provide outstanding fall foliage colors ranging from deep orange to scarlet or maroon. Individual plants have a dense, cascading growth habit and display noticeable reddish twigs in winter.

Sweetspire grows naturally in moist, swampy conditions, but it will also grow well in rich, well-drained garden soils. It is essentially trouble free and establishes itself quickly in the garden. Plants will grow 3–5 ft. tall and twice as wide, creating large colonies of lush growth. Full sun or partial shade is best for good flower production and fall color.

Virginia sweetspire is a versatile plant that can be used in many landscape situations. It is a very useful plant for naturalizing in woodland settings, mass plantings, foundation plantings, informal hedges, and areas of the garden with poor drainage. Virginia sweetspire is a superb flowering shrub for the home garden— especially some of the new choice garden varieties. It will rarely disappoint, even in the most challenging of landscapes. Hardy from Zones 5–9.

NOTABLE VARIETIES

'Henry's Garnet'. One of the best and most popular varieties available, with flowers up to 6 in. long and deep red or purple fall color. This selection is extremely cold and heat tolerant.

Little Henry ('Sprich'). A compact, low-growing variety that will grow 2–3 ft. tall with an equal spread. Beautiful red purple fall color and 3–4 in. white flowers. It is excellent for small gardens.

The deep reddish maroon fall foliage of 'Henry's Garnet'

'Merlot'. Another compact grower with excellent red fall foliage color.

'Saturnalia'. This selection offers yellow, bright orange, or red fall foliage color. Provides very bright colors in autumn that will liven up any garden.

{ *Jasminum nudiflorum*
Winter jasmine

This winter bloomer provides a glimpse of spring in winter with small, trumpetlike, bright yellow flowers. Although the flowers are not fragrant, they will sporadically open along older stems for several months and provide a consistent show. The low, mounded, arching, green stems also provide winter interest. Individual plants form a twiggy mass of stems maturing to 4 ft. tall and double the spread. In spring, small, dark, glossy, green leaves unfold and remain until fall.

Winter jasmine is easy to grow and will thrive in moist, well-drained soil and full sun or partial shade. It adapts well to poor soils and is fairly drought tolerant. Plants may need to be rejuvenated every few years, and this can be achieved by cutting the plant down to 6 in. in early spring. This practice will keep the plants dense and productive.

Winter jasmine is very effective for mid to late winter and early spring interest. It can be used in mass plantings or foundation plantings. It is particularly effective when cascading over rock walls and along slopes. This very interesting and adaptable plant is cold hardy from Zones 6–10, possibly hardy in Zone 5 in a sheltered location.

Kerria in flower

{ *Kerria japonica*
Japanese kerria

Japanese kerria is a spring-flowering shrub with circular, bright yellow flowers produced in profusion. Although it may be difficult to see the family resemblance, this early- to mid-spring-flowering shrub is a member of the rose family and is also known as Japanese rose. The upright growth habit, thin, olive green twigs, and sharply serrated leaves also provide ornamental value. Kerria exhibits showy single or double flowers depending on the variety you choose. This interesting shrub frequently reblooms throughout the summer and has a muted yellow fall foliage color.

Japanese kerria prefers moist, well-drained, acidic soils and partial shade. It is remarkably shade tolerant and will perform admirably in full shade. This flowering shrub flowers on the previous year's growth, and pruning can be done soon after flowering. Shrubs that are performing poorly can be selectively pruned or rejuvenated in early spring. Do not overfertilize this plant, as it may reduce flower production.

Kerria will grow 3–6 ft. tall and 6 ft. or more wide at maturity; however, it can easily be maintained as a smaller shrub with proper pruning. Kerria can be used in mass plantings, small groupings, and in shade gardens as an accent plant. It is also a great companion plant to shade-loving perennials. It will definitely brighten up a dark, dull area of the garden. Hardy from Zones 4–9 and performs best in a sheltered location in extremely cold climates.

NOTABLE VARIETIES

'Albescens'. The single flowers are a creamy, pale yellow or off white. A nice selection if a paler flower color is desired.

'Golden Guinea'. Large, showy golden single flowers are a nice contrast to the rich, green leaves.

'Picta'. The creamy white variegated leaves provide a beautiful accent to a shade garden. Although this selection will also display single, yellow flowers, it is more often used as an effective accent foliage plant.

'Pleniflora'. This is a double-flowering form with deeply ruffled, rounded, yellow flowers.

'Shannon'. A large, single-flowering type with bright yellow blooms early in the season.

{ *Kolkwitzia amabilis*
Beautybush

Beautybush has earned its name from the masses of beautiful pink, trumpetlike flowers that are displayed in mid spring. The large bunches of tightly arranged flowers transform into puffs of hairy fruit capsules late in the summer season. This upright shrub can grow 6–10 ft. tall and forms a dense branching habit. The small, medium-green, pointed leaves turn yellowish to red in the fall.

Beautybush is easy to grow and will thrive in moist well-drained soils and full sun. It is very adaptable to varying soil pH and is drought tolerant once established. Regular selective pruning to remove older stems is recommended to maximize flower production and vigor. If plants get too overgrown, a severe pruning in the early spring will rejuvenate older shrubs, but flowers will be sacrificed for one year. However, flower production the following year will be impressive.

This large, flowering shrub is best suited as a stand-alone plant in the home landscape. It requires plenty of room and can easily outgrow its assigned garden space if sited incorrectly. Since it forms a very dense mass of growth, it can also be used as a tall screen or informal hedge. Hardy from Zones 4–8.

'Pink Cloud' has profuse masses of light pink flowers, which form a cloud of magnificent color.

Crape myrtle flower

{ *Lagerstroemia indica*
Crape myrtle

Crape myrtle has long been considered a desirable shrub for the warmer climates of the southeastern United States. The clusters of frilly, papery flowers can reach 8 in. long or more and 5 in. wide. Flower color is variable and can range from white, pink, lavender, purple, and deep red. This plant will produce masses of flowers in mid to late summer and into the fall. After the flowers have finished, bunches of green, round capsulelike fruit will form. In spring, the newly emerging leaves will often unfold a bronzy red color before maturing to glossy medium to dark green. In the autumn, the leaves change to brilliant shades of yellow, orange, and red. But crape myrtle is also valued for its outstanding smooth, multicolored, flaking bark that provides exceptional interest all year especially in the winter.

Crape myrtles are very diverse and can range in size from 18 in. to 25 ft., depending on the variety you choose. Most often this shrub grows as an upright, multistemmed shrub or small tree. It does particularly well in hot, dry climates and tends not to grow as large in northern areas. It is very adaptable to many types of soils but thrives in moist, well-drained soil and full sun. A crape myrtle sited in poorly drained or wet soils and shade will perform poorly. Winter fertilization will help increase flower production and vigor. The long-

believed myth that crape myrtles are not hardy in the northern states is false. They are hardy from Zones 6–9 but do benefit from shelter in colder climates where extended periods of cold temperatures may exist. A light layer of mulch or pine straw will also help to protect the roots from fluctuating soil temperatures and varying degrees of moisture.

Since crape myrtle blooms are on current season's growth, pruning right after blooms fade may encourage a second flush of flowers. This technique is more effective in warmer climates with mild, extended growing seasons. In addition, wispy sucker growth from the base of the plant should be removed. If considerable pruning is needed, selective pruning while the plant is dormant in late winter will produce good results. Pruning large shrubs back to very thick stems or main trunks should be avoided since that will often cause a flush of long, pliable, weak stems. Instead, the canopy can be thinned and top growth cut back to branches no thicker than your pinky finger. To train taller-growing crape myrtle varieties as small trees, prune off any young, spindly, or thin branches from the lower part of the plant, leaving several mature, main stems.

Crape myrtle is an integral part of landscapes in the southern United States. It is slowly gaining in popularity in the Northeast as well. It is versatile in the landscape and can be used as a small specimen tree or large shrub, mass planting, informal hedge, screen, and is a valuable accent to flowering shrubs or perennials. It is important to decide which type of crape myrtle will suit you best, as each variety has a different flower color, form, and garden function. Undoubtedly, you

Crape myrtle bark

will find an appropriate color and size that is right for your garden.

NOTABLE VARIETIES

Below is a very modest sampling of the many cultivated varieties available for the home garden.

'Acoma'. A semi-dwarf selection growing 5–10 ft. high and wide with white flowers and light gray bark.

Dynamite ('Whit II'). A spectacular red-flowering form that will provide a burst of color in the summer landscape. This is a large grower that can exceed 15 ft. in height.

'Hopi'. This shrubby crape myrtle will produce light pink flowers and variations of brown-gray bark.

'Lipan'. An interesting variety with lavender flowers and beige/white bark. This variety typically grows as a large shrub or small tree, to 15–20 ft.

'Natchez'. A beautiful, large-growing variety with pure white flowers and cinnamon brown bark. Excellent as a small to medium-sized tree for a home landscape, provided adequate room is available.

'Pocomoke'. A superb low-growing form that will only grow 2–3 ft. tall with a slightly greater spread. The lush foliage and deep pink flowers make this plant ideal for the home landscape. It can be used in groupings, foundation plantings, along the edges of flower borders, and as a companion plant to perennials.

'Tuscarora'. Attractive dark coral pink flowers are a nice contrast to the light brown, smooth bark. This variety can get large and is easily trained as a small tree.

'Zuni'. This semi-dwarf variety has a dense growth habit, showy lavender flowers, and gray-brown bark.

{ *Lespedeza thunbergii*
Bush clover, thunberg lespedeza

This choice shrub offers masses of deep pink, 6 in. long, loose flower clusters on the tips of each branch. The cascading growth habit and showy flowers droop to the ground, creating a waterfall effect. The lacey, blue-green foliage also adds a fine texture to the landscape. The graceful, vase-shaped growth habit of lespedeza will reach 3–5 ft. in one season.

For best flower production, lespedeza should be pruned to within 6 in. of the ground in late winter to encourage a new flush of growth and flowers in the spring and summer. This will also keep the plants healthy and vigorous. Lespedeza will thrive in hot, dry conditions and full sun but will also perform very well in moist, well-drained soils and light shade. It is a true performer in hot, dry areas with poor, sandy soils.

As a cutback shrub, thunberg lespedeza is excellent addition to a perennial border and in groupings with other summer-blooming shrubs. The fine foliage texture and profuse flowers provide unique late-summer interest. Hardy from Zones 5–8.

NOTABLE VARIETIES

'Avalanche'. Pure white flowers provide a snowy white display in midsummer.

'Gibraltar'. Beautiful masses of deep rosy purple flowers are quite handsome.

'Spring Grove'. Attractive rose-purple flowers and a graceful growth habit make this an interesting addition to the landscape.

© Richard Weis III

Neillia sinensis in flower

{ *Neillia sinensis*
Chinese neillia

Chinese neillia is a choice flowering shrub that is rarity in the home landscape. It is sometimes found in the collector's garden, where it will complement other unusual garden treasures. The small groups of pink flowers dangle off the irregular-growing stems in mid spring. The lush, deep green, serrated leaves provide excellent texture during the summer. The tightly arranged stems form a zigzag pattern that is interesting all year, especially when the shrub sheds its leaves in the fall. The bark on older, mature stems will exfoliate, adding another interesting dimension to this underutilized plant.

Neillia will grow to 6 ft. wide and tall but can grow larger in optimum conditions. The densely growing branches create a thicket, making it difficult to see through even during the winter months. They prefer moist, well-drained soil and full sun or partial shade. Pruning can be done soon after flowering to keep plants maintained. However, selective pruning in early spring is best to stimulate healthy plant growth. Neillia is an adaptable plant but performs best in cooler climates of the northern United States.

Neillia needs room but will function as a natural screen, mass planting, informal hedge, and as a background plant. While this species is not readily obtainable, it will serve a distinctive role and present a unique presence unlike most of the shrubs commonly available today. This is a choice plant that can likely be acquired from a mail order plant nursery. Hardy from Zones 5–7.

{ *Philadelphus* spp.
Mockorange
Philadelphus coronarius (sweet mockorange)

Sweet mockorange inherited its name from the sweet, intoxicatingly fragrant white flowers that appear in spring. The dark green leaves provide a pleasant canvas for the clusters of white blooms. The reddish brown stems provide interest in the winter, especially against a blanket of snow.

This European native is quite adaptable but does best in full sun or partial shade and moist well-drained soils. It will tolerate poor soils and considerable shade but flower production will be reduced. Selective pruning in late winter is recommended to remove weak or less productive stems. If your shrubs are too overgrown, a nonselective, rejuvenation pruning can be done to renovate the plant. Sweet mockorange will grow to 10–12 ft. in height and spread but typically does not reach such large sizes unless fully mature.

Mockorange is best sited where you and your garden guests can enjoy the pleasant fragrance. Mass plantings, groupings, and informal hedges are good uses for this plant. Hardy from Zones 4–8.

OTHER NOTABLE VARIETIES

Below is a list of a few select mockorange varieties derived from several different species.

P. coronarius 'Aureus'. The foliage is striking yellow fading to chartreuse-yellow over time. The foliage color makes this variety ideal for accents in partly shaded areas in the garden. This variety is more effective in cooler climates with less heat and humidity since the leaf color is less likely to fade. It is very effective when used to brighten up rather color-challenged areas in the garden.

P. coronarius 'Variegatus'. Creamy white leaf edges make this worthy shrub a good accent plant in a partially shaded area of the garden.

P. x *lemoinei* 'Innocence'. This variety is derived from a hybrid and is one of the best mockoranges for fragrance. It is a unique selection, with leaves splashed with off-white variegation. Good as an accent plant for sun or partially shaded areas.

P. x *virginalis* 'Minnesota Snowflake'. A hybrid mockorange with white, double flowers with a ruffled appearance and pleasant fragrance.

P. 'Snowbelle'. A hybrid mockorange with a compact growth habit to 4 ft. tall and masses of small, white, fragrant double flowers.

{ *Physocarpus opulifolius*
Common ninebark

This North American native naturally grows from Quebec, Canada, to the eastern and Midwestern United States. It is used as an ornamental garden shrub and looks similar to a viburnum, but it is actually a member of the rose family. Ninebark has white or light pink flowers in mid to late spring and medium green leaves in the summer. Mature specimens will offer winter interest since the bark on the older branches will peel off in brown sheets. Although it is not a particularly overwhelming shrub in the landscape, there are several new varieties that make attractive foliage plants. Ninebark does offer several seasons of interest and is a reliable performer in the garden.

Ninebark, like viburnum and mockorange, is a very adaptable shrub, growing well in various soils. It is not pH dependent and can also tolerate poor, dry soils. It thrives in full sun or partial shade and moist, well-drained soil. Rejuvenation pruning to 12 in. in early spring will stimulate this shrub to grow several feet in one season. If left unpruned. this shrub can reach 10 ft. tall but can be maintained with selective pruning.

Ninebark has gained in popularity over the past few years since several new varieties have emerged with purple or yellow foliage. These interesting "accent" plants should be pruned to 6 in. from the ground annually to encourage deep, intense colors. Like

Bush cinquefoil flower

smokebush (*Cotinus*), this plant functions well as a "curback shrub" and is also very useful in mass plantings, shrub borders, and when mixed with perennials. An extremely cold hardy plant, it grows in Zones 2–7.

NOTABLE VARIETIES

'Dart's Gold'. A compact grower with golden foliage in spring fading to a yellow-green over time. Plants will grow 4–5 ft. tall with a similar spread. A very nice accent plant when mixed with dark foliage plants.

'Nugget'. Similar to 'Dart's Gold', it is another fine yellow leaf form worth trying. Great compact growth habit.

Diablo ('Monlo'). Foliage is a deep purple in spring, fading to a purplish green as leaves mature. The bold, robust leaves provide great texture and color in the landscape during the summer months. In hot, humid climates, the purple pigment in the leaves frequently weakens. Still, it is a very hardy and useful accent plant in the right situation.

{ *Potentilla fruticosa*
Bush cinquefoil

Bush cinquefoil is a pleasant little shrub with several worthwhile garden attributes. It is a widely distributed native, growing in many regions of the Northern Hemisphere. The small, bright yellow flowers resemble buttercups and open in early summer and continue until the arrival of cool temperatures in fall. The delicate but colorful single flowers come in an assortment of colors, depending on the variety that is selected. The dainty leaves unfold a soft, silvery green and mature to medium green. Bush cinquefoil's growth habit is mounded and dense with shrubs growing 2–4 ft. in height with an equal spread.

This carefree plant is not particularly demanding and can yield delightful aesthetic rewards with colorful blooms and interesting foliage. It prefers full sun and moist, well-drained soil. Yet bush cinquefoil will also do surprisingly well in poor, sandy soils, high pH soils, and hot, dry conditions. Plants can easily be kept dense and productive with selective or rejuvenation pruning in late winter or early spring.

Bush cinquefoil can be used in a wide range of landscape situations including mass plantings, foundation plantings, as an edging plant, companion to perennial plantings, low hedge, and is especially effective near the seashore. Hardy from Zones 2–7. Performs best in cooler climates.

NOTABLE VARIETIES

'Abbotswood'. Masses of white flowers look like mini single roses. The blue-green foliage and dense 3 ft. by 3 ft. habit is also very attractive.

'Gold Drop'. This variety produces loads of deep yellow flowers and a dwarf growth habit.

'Primrose Beauty'. Primrose yellow flowers fade to pale yellow with age. A very attractive shrub with grayish green foliage.

'Tangerine'. This European variety offers bright yellow to orange flowers.

{ *Rhus typhina*
Staghorn sumac

There are about 150 species of sumac, some of which are native to America. This diverse group of plants is a vital part of the natural woodland and seashore environment. Its most impressionable attributes are the spikes of red fruit and exquisite orange to fiery red fall foliage color.

Sumac is well known as a very durable shrub or small tree that is especially suitable in barren, poor soils and harsh, dry conditions. As the plants mature, they develop an irregular, picturesque growth habit that is very artistic. Because of that quality, this plant can be a conversation piece for all four seasons.

Although there are several species that will perform well in the garden, staghorn sumac is the most popular and most readily available. It has a large leaf extending one to two feet long made up of many smaller leaflets. The bright green leaf changes brilliant shades of yellow, orange, and red in the fall and is sure to impress plant lovers throughout the autumn.

Staghorn sumac has male and female flowers on separate plants (dioecious), a characteristic similar to holly. In the summer, sumac will exhibit large, cone-shaped, greenish yellow flower clusters that transform into deep red fruit in the fall. The fruit will persist into the winter and are an excellent source of high protein food for migratory birds. The irregular growth patterns of staghorn sumac become very interesting with age. The thick stems are covered with velvety hairs and resemble a deer's antlers, and this soft texture provides great interest during the winter.

This resilient native prefers full sun and moist, well-drained soil but will adapt to almost any landscape situation. It will thrive in hot, dry conditions and sandy soils. Although staghorn sumac will grow into a small tree, it can easily be maintained as a small- to medium-sized shrub with regular pruning. The plants can be selectively pruned in late winter to accomplish this goal.

Staghorn sumac is especially effective in seashore conditions and highly exposed areas. It is also excellent as a companion plant to smaller flowering shrubs and perennials. Hardy from Zones 4–8.

'Laciniata' is a female variety that has finely cut, fernlike leaves. It is a very delicate-looking shrub that is useful in mass plantings, naturalistic gardens, and perennial borders.

{ *Rosa* spp.
{ Rose

For centuries, roses have been a vital part of gardening throughout the globe. They are one of the most recognizable and desirable flowering plants in all facets of the horticultural world. Roses are admired for their beautiful fragrant flowers, which come in a rainbow of colors, ornamental fruit known as rose hips, and handsome glossy foliage. There are several types of rose flowers, including a single type, which reveals the open center of the flower, and the traditional double flower which has a ruffled appearance. The flowers are coveted for their intoxicating fragrance, which few gardeners can resist. The rose hips are oval or globe-shaped fruit that can range in size and color but are usually red or orange when ripe.

In general, roses require regular care to keep them healthy and productive. Many varieties are susceptible

Knockout rose in the landscape

to an assortment of diseases and pest problems, such as aphids, spider mites, midge, black spot, rust, and powdery mildew. Black spot is one of the most prevalent and common diseases of roses, causing small, black spots on the leaves. Badly infested plants may defoliate, and if shrubs are healthy they will produce new leaves. The severity of black spot depends on many factors such as environmental conditions, varieties, and even region of the country the plant is growing. For example, roses growing in the Pacific Northwest region of the United States may not have the same types or degree of disease and pest problems that you might encounter in the southeastern United States.

Although many of these disease and pest problems can be treated with pesticides, there are a many other environmentally sound alternatives to address this issue. Among these alternatives, the most effective is proper plant selection. Significant research has yielded dozens of new and exciting varieties of landscape roses that offer a shrubby habit, improved flowering characteristics, and reasonably good pest resistance. These attributes result in less maintenance and more enjoyment.

If pesticides are needed, careful research should be done to select the best product for a specific problem. Before you apply pesticides, you should consult with a local county extension agent or horticultural professional.

The cultivated varieties listed below are hardy in Zones 4–8, with a few exceptions. In addition, these low-growing or shrubby roses are excellent as low informal hedges, mass plantings, and foundation

Knockout in flower

Scarlet Meidiland in flower

plantings, and they will work well with herbaceous plants. They thrive in well-drained, moist soils and full sun but are reasonably tolerant of poor soils and drought conditions. Spring and/or fall fertilization and regular watering will also benefit shrub roses. Shrub roses can be pruned in the early spring to thin out older stems, leaving the younger, stronger stems to grow.

The listing below is a modest offering of some of the more choice rose selections available for the home garden. Please note that while in most case throughout this book, cultivated variety names are listed with single quotes around each name (i.e., *Rosa* 'The Fairy'),

some trademarked or registered names are more common and identifiable on the market. Therefore, several of the roses listed below indicate these common trade or registered names with cultivated variety names in parentheses.

NOTABLE VARIETIES

Alba Meidiland ('Meiflopan'). Large clusters of small, white flowers with a slight fragrance. This low-growing plant has a nice, cascading growth habit reaching 2 ½ ft. tall and 6 ft. wide.

Bonica ('Mediopmonac'). This upright grower offers lush, dark green foliage and medium pink, double flowers. Plants will grow to 4 ft. dense mounds.

Carefree Delight ('Meipotal'). These hardy, compact growers provide attractive single pink blooms all summer. Plants will grow to 3 ½ ft. tall with a similar spread.

Carefree Sunshine ('Radsun'). This unique shrub

has golden yellow flowers and a compact, 3–4 ft. dense growth habit.

Carefree Wonder ('Meipitac'). A very popular variety with interesting shades of pink blended into each semi-double flower. The dense, neat growth habit will reach 4 ft. in height.

Flower Carpet series. These ground-hugging varieties have glossy green leaves and vibrant flower colors ranging from yellow, red, pink, coral, and white. Excellent in mass plantings, along the edge of a flowerbed or walkway, and on embankments.

Knockout ('Rodrazz'). An excellent variety with a name that speaks for itself. Cherry red or deep pink blooms will dazzle you with vibrant colors. The beautiful, dark green foliage and compact growth habit are also very impressive. Truly a knockout!

R. chinensis 'Mutabilis'. A shrub rose to 6 ft. tall and wide with beautiful multicolored flowers changing from bright yellow to salmon to deep pink. This plant also has very beautiful blue-green foliage but is susceptible to black spot. It is still a good performer and worthy of planting in the garden. Excellent in Zones 7–8.

Pink Meidiland ('Meipoque'). The single pink flowers with white centers emerge in spring and flowering will continue into the fall. The dense, upright growth habit will reach 4 ft. high and 2 ½ ft. wide. After flowering, red rose hips will persist, adding winter interest.

Scarlet Meidiland ('Meikrotal'). This variety provides clusters of small, scarlet red, double flowers in early summer with blooming continuing through fall. This variety will grow 3 ft. high by 6 ft. wide and is great for a dense informal hedge or mass planting.

'Seafoam'. An older, established variety with small, creamy white, double flowers in profusion beginning in early summer and continuing sporadically into the fall. This vigorous grower will grow 3 ft. high by 6 ft. wide with a beautiful cascading growth habit.

'The Fairy'. A very reliable performer with beautiful, pink, double flowers in midsummer and a dense, low-growing habit. The glossy green leaves are also

Climbing rose Scarlet Rambler in flower

attractive. Individual plants range in size from 2–3 ft. up to 4 ft. in height with an equal spread.

CLIMBERS

There are many climbing roses to choose from that will grow on a trellis, fence, arbor, or even in other shrubs or trees. This glorious effect of fragrant masses of color cascading from above is the most attractive element of theses vigorous vines. If sited correctly, these garden gems can act as a main focal point in the garden. To keep your climbers healthy and vigorous, it is beneficial to selectively prune rose plants in spring to remove older, less-productive stems. Some judicious pruning can be done in the summer as well. The younger stems that remain will continue to flourish and yield masses of blooms.

NOTABLE VARIETIES

Here is just a sample of some common varieties worth trying.

'Dortmund'. A vigorous grower with clusters of small bright red flowers with white centers.

'New Dawn'. A good performer with clusters of delicate, soft pink flowers.

'Zephirine Drouhin'. An old-fashioned variety with showy, fragrant, cerise pink flowers.

{ *Sambucus* spp.
{ Elder

Elder is a multistemmed shrub with creamy white, flat-topped flowers that appear in midsummer followed by reddish black fruit in late summer and fall.

Sambucus Black Beauty in flower

The fruit is a desirable food source for birds. The medium green, fernlike leaves provide a lush, medium texture in the landscape. There is an assortment of foliage colors and types, depending on the cultivated variety chosen.

Elder is an upright shrub reaching 8–12 ft. in height with a 6–8 ft. spread. They do best in moist soils, but certain species are remarkably tolerant of drier soil conditions. Full sun is preferable, but elders are also quite shade tolerant. This shrub requires regular pruning to keep it dense and manageable, especially if growing in shade. Plants can be pruned in early spring while still dormant or right after flowering.

There are several species of elders that play important roles as ornamentals in the garden. Recent new introductions have made this plant more desirable in the landscape. It can be used in groupings, shrub borders, and woodland gardens and is also excellent as a background plant when mixed with other flowering plants. In addition, new, variegated gold and purple leaf forms are ideal cutback shrubs. Prune plants down to 6–12 in. each spring to encourage new, vigorous growth and rich vibrant foliage colors.

Sambucus canadensis (American elder)

This widespread shrub is native from eastern and central Canada to the southern United States. The white, flat-topped flowers emerge in profusion in midsummer, followed by purple-black fruit in late summer and early fall. The fruit is edible and will be devoured by birds.

American elder thrives in moist, rich soil and full sun or partial shade. It is well suited for areas that are poorly drained and will also tolerate sandy soils. American elder is well suited for commercial use for naturalizing and highway plantings as well as the home landscape. 'Laciniata' is an attractive garden variety with deeply cut leaves providing a fine, lacey texture. Hardy from Zones 3–9. In Zone 3, this shrub is best sited in a sheltered location.

'Aurea' has bright golden yellow foliage and white flowers. Very striking in partial shade.

Sambucus nigra (European elder)

This large shrub or small tree offers white flowers in summer and clusters of black fruit in the fall. Many new varieties have made this species highly sought-after in the cultivated garden. The varieties listed below tend to grow more slowly than the species. Hardy from Zones 5–7.

NOTABLE VARIETIES

'Aurea'. Golden yellow leaves fade over time. Excellent in a partly shaded area of the garden as an accent plant for a splash of color.

Black Beauty ('Gerda'). A variety that originated in England with beautiful, dark purple foliage and bright pink flowers in summer. Although the flowers are attractive, this plant is very effective as a cutback shrub to encourage dense, deep purple foliage color. A great accent plant when mixed with other foliage plants with gold or variegated leaves.

'Madonna'. Leaf edges splashed with yellow variegation. An attractive accent plant for light shade.

'Pulverulenta'. Leaves speckled and splashed with white variegation. A very attractive accent plant suitable for a partly shaded area in the garden.

Sambucus racemosa (European red elder)

This multistemmed shrub has an upright growth habit to 8–10 ft. The yellowish white flowers emerge in late spring and early summer and are followed by red fruit clusters. 'Sutherland Gold' is a common variety with bright golden yellow, finely cut leaves. It seems to perform best in cooler climates, where it will not experience extreme heat and humidity. For best foliage color, cut the plants down to 6 in. in early spring every few years. Hardy from Zones 4–7.

{ *Sorbaria sorbifolia*
False spirea

False spirea is a large, spreading shrub, growing 8–10 ft. tall and wide. In early to midsummer it displays white, plumelike flowers that will persist for several weeks. The handsome, textured foliage is tinged red as it emerges and eventually matures to dark green.

False spirea thrives in moist, organic soils and prefers full sun or partial shade. It is very adaptable to soil types and varying soil pH levels. False spirea flowers on new growth, so pruning should be done in the early spring before the plant leafs out.

This interesting but somewhat obscure flowering shrub is not well known in commerce and will likely be found at a specialty plant nursery. It is a shrub worthy of cultivation and will offer aesthetic value and function in landscapes with adequate space. False spirea is suited for mass plantings, shrub borders, and background plantings in areas where it has room to spread. It is a very hardy plant, growing from Zones 2–7, and may also adapt to Zone 8 with proper siting.

Spiraea spp.
Spirea

Spirea is a popular group of flowering shrubs that have been an important part of gardening since the late 1800s. Like hydrangea, rhododendron, and lilac, spirea has earned the reputation as a hardy, colorful, old-fashioned shrub. Spirea's popularity stems from its ability to adapt to many different landscape situations and perform very well. They offer showy small bouquets of white or pink flowers that are easily recognizable to even the novice gardener.

Spirea is not without faults and can fall prey to several damaging insects such as aphids, scale, and caterpillars. However, even with these potential problems, spirea exhibits remarkable resiliency. They perform best in full sun or partial shade and well drained, loamy soils but will tolerate many types of soils except those that are wet or soggy. Spirea species either bloom in spring or summer. As a general rule, spring-blooming spireas should be pruned after flowering and summer-blooming types should be pruned while dormant in early spring. For this reason it is important to know which type of spirea you have growing in the garden.

The spireas listed below are suitable for the home garden because they possess rather dwarf growth habits and excellent aesthetic value. Spireas offer versatile landscape function and can be used in mass plantings, foundation plantings, perennial borders, and are excellent as low edging plants or informal hedges. Hardy from Zones 3–8 depending on the species.

Spiraea x *bumalda* (bumald spirea)

This dwarf shrub forms a dense mound of growth reaching 3–4 ft. high with a similar spread. The new reddish purple leaves unfold in spring and change to dark green with age. The small, flat-topped flower bouquets range in color from white to deep pink in early to midsummer. Often plants will sporadically bloom into the fall.

Bumald spirea is very adaptable but does best in loamy, well-drained soils and full sun. Since it flowers on the most current season's growth, pruning before leaves emerge in the spring is recommended. Plants can be pruned down to 6 in. and will grow several feet in one season while displaying a mass of flowers. Once the flowers have faded, prune them off, which often encourages another flush of blooms.

Bumald spirea is very functional in the home garden and can be used in mass plantings, foundation plantings, shrub borders, and as an informal, low hedge. It is also a great companion plant to herbaceous plants. Hardy from Zones 3–8.

NOTABLE VARIETIES

'Anthony Waterer'. This popular variety is an improvement over the species with the new foliage tinged reddish purple and rosy pink flower clusters. In the autumn, foliage will often display attractive shades of red.

'Goldflame'. This low-growing shrub offers mounds of yellowish green leaves with reddish tips on the new growth. The foliage provides an effective canvas for the bright pink flowers. Because of its color and texture, 'Goldflame' can be a useful accent plant when mixed with other dwarf shrubs.

'Goldmound'. A hybrid spirea with a low-growing, mounded habit and golden yellow foliage fading to chartreuse green with age. The small pink flowers develop during the summer months, and fall foliage is typically an attractive orange-red.

Spiraea japonica (Japanese spirea)

This upright, rounded shrub will grow to 5 ft. tall. It has showy, pink flowers in summer and dark green foliage. There are many dwarf selections of this species that are primarily derivatives of a naturally

'Goldmound' spirea in the garden

occurring miniature variety listed as var. *alpina.*

There are also several worthy selections that have emerged from hybrids between bumald spirea and

'Ogon' spirea in full bloom

Japanese spirea. As with bumald spirea, annual early spring pruning will encourage showy summer blooms on Japanese spirea. Hardy from Zones 4–8.

NOTABLE VARIETIES

'Little Princess'. A truly dwarf plant, growing to merely 2 ½ ft. tall. The lush, green leaves and abundant pink flowers make this very desirable plant for a garden with limited space. Excellent for rock gardens and in combination with other compact growers.

'Shirobana' ('Shibori'). This in an interesting variety, exhibiting a combination of white, pink, and rose-colored flowers. The flowers will continue sporadically into the fall. The beautifully textured leaves provide interest from spring until late fall.

Spiraea nipponica 'Snowmound' ('Snowmound' spirea)

'Snowmound' forms a dense, upright, mounded growth habit reaching 4–5 ft. high and equally as wide. The pure white, bouquetlike clusters of flowers appear in mass along the dense branches. This attractive shrub typically blooms in late spring and early summer. The deep blue-green leaves are a handsome attribute during the summer months. This species is hardy from Zones 4–7 but can be grown in Zones 3 and 8 with additional care and specific siting.

Spiraea thunbergii (thunberg spirea)

Thunberg spirea is an old-fashioned shrub with a graceful, fine texture. It provides an impressive show in early to mid spring, with masses of delicate, white flowers. The upright, cascading growth habit and small, thin leaves give this plant a wispy, broomlike appearance. The fine leaves develop a light to medium green color, making the plant quite a nice accent in the landscape. This species flowers on previous season's growth, and modest pruning can be done after flowers have finished. Selective pruning in the early spring can also be done to keep plants vigorous and productive. However, spring pruning will compromise some flowers for one season. Hardy from Zones 4–8.

'Ogon' is a selection with a soft, yellow leaves that change to pale green. It's a very effective variety when used an accent plant or in mass plantings. This particular variety is useful in partially shaded areas of the garden.

{ *Stephanandra incisa*
Cutleaf stephanandra

This graceful, mounded shrub is one of the elite of the shrub world. It has many interesting horticultural attributes to offer the home garden. The densely matted branches form a rounded, spreading habit. The small, finely cut leaves emerge reddish bronze before changing to medium green during the summer. The leaves eventually change to shades of yellow, orange, and red in the fall, but this transformation is not usually overwhelming. In mid to late spring, small clusters of white flowers open and last for several weeks. Although not particularly overpowering individually, the delicate flower clusters in mass provide a discernible display. This shrub also exhibits winter interest, with conspicuous light brown stems and a cascading branching structure.

Stephanandra is a medium-to-fast-growing shrub growing 4–8 ft. high with an equal spread. It adapts well to many different landscape situations but thrives in moist, well-drained, acidic soil. For best performance, this shrub should be sited in full sun or partial shade. Regular pruning is not often needed, but pruning poorly shaped shrubs to 6 in. from the ground can easily rejuvenate them. Trimming or shearing into formal shapes is not recommended, as it will ruin the shrub's natural, graceful growth habit.

Stephanandra is ideal in mass plantings, small groupings, as an informal hedge, and even suitable as a screening plant due to its dense habit. Hardy from Zones 4–7, but it will do reasonably well in Zone 8 if it receives adequate moisture and a sheltered location.

'Crispa' is a charming, compact variety with a low, creeping habit. This dwarf form will reach 2–3 ft. in height with a wider spread. It is very effective as a groundcover, mass planting, and edging plant.

Stephanandra incisa 'Crispa' foliage

{ *Syringa* spp.
Lilac

Syringa vulgaris (common lilac)

The traditional common lilac is one of the most popular and beloved flowering shrubs in the home garden. The masses of white, pink, purple, and violet flowers exude an intoxicating fragrance that is rivaled by few plants. But there are several reasons why this species is not the most ideal shrub for the home landscape. First, common lilac can easily outgrow small spaces and will reach heights of 10–15 ft. once established. Common lilac is also prone to several pests, including leaf spots, powdery mildew, lilac borer, and scale. It performs best in well-drained soil with near neutral (7.0) pH levels.

However, there is a whole new breed of dwarf and semi-dwarf shrubby lilacs that exhibit amazing adaptability and function in the confines of the home garden. These densely branched shrubs offer masses of pink or purple flowers, beautiful foliage, and dense growth characteristics. Admittedly, these shrub lilacs do not possess the same size, scale, and bold beauty that the common lilac exhibits, but they are delightful and valuable in their own way.

While lilacs benefit from neutral (7.0) or higher pH soils, the dwarf lilacs listed in this book will perform well in a wide range of soil types and pH levels. These lilacs prefer moist, well-drained soil and full sun, although they will tolerate partial shade. Significant pruning is not often needed on a regular basis, but occasional selective pruning to keep plants productive is important. Lilacs bloom on previous season's growth, so any severe pruning in early spring will result in reduced flowers the first season after pruning.

Because of their dense, spreading, and relatively compact growth habit, these shrubby lilacs are best in mass plantings, foundation plantings, informal hedges, shrub borders, and are excellent garden companions to herbaceous plantings.

Syringa meyeri (Meyer lilac)

Meyer lilac forms a dense, mounded growth habit that can reach 4–8 ft. in height with a slightly larger spread. The small, purple flowers provide a profusion of color in mid to late spring. The flowers are fragrant although not as sweetly scented as common lilac. The small, glossy green leaves provide an attractive, fine texture in the landscape.

Meyer lilac is one of the easiest and most adaptable lilacs to grow. It prefers full sun but will tolerate partial shade. It is also pest resistant and drought tolerant and will perform well in many landscape situations. Hardy from Zones 3–7.

'Palibin' is a dwarf selection growing only 4–5 ft. tall with a slightly wider spread. The purple flower buds open to light pink flowers. It is a very good lilac for the home garden.

Syringa microphylla (littleaf lilac)

Littleleaf lilac is an old-fashioned lilac with a wide-spreading growth habit, attractive foliage, and beautiful pink flowers. Individual plants can grow 6 ft. tall and twice as wide, but only when plants are quite old. The small clusters of lilac-colored flowers offer a sweet fragrance in mid to late spring. These beautiful shrubs will often sporadically rebloom in early fall. Another attractive feature of this fine shrub is the small, fuzzy leaves that are soft to the touch. As littleleaf lilac matures, it forms arching, graceful branches that will spill to the ground.

Littleleaf lilac is resistant to most of the common lilac problems such as powdery mildew. It is also very adaptable to many environmental conditions but prefers moist, well-drained soil and full sun. Selective pruning to remove older, unproductive branches will ensure that plants remain healthy, productive, and somewhat compact. This plant should not be sheared since it would ruin the graceful, semi-weeping growth habit.

Littleleaf lilac is a very effective informal hedge, mass planting, or specimen plant, as long as it is given room to spread. Hardy from Zones 4–7. This species may also perform fairly well in Zone 8 if adequate moisture is provided. Partial shade in hot, humid climates is also beneficial.

'Superba' is a great variety that produces masses of deep pink flowers in spring. It is a really terrific performer.

Syringa patula 'Miss Kim' ('Miss Kim' lilac)

This handsome shrub has a rounded, upright growth habit to 6 ft. tall and wide. The 3 in. clusters of purple flower buds open to fragrant, icy lavender-blue flowers in mid to late spring. The glossy green leaves are also quite striking and turn deep reddish purple in fall. Hardy from Zones 4–7, and to Zone 8 with additional care.

Close up of littleleaf lilac flowers

Littleleaf lilac in flower

Syringa laciniata (cutleaf lilac)

This unusual species has exquisite lilac-colored flowers in spring and dark green, deeply serrated leaves. This shrub can grow to 6 ft. tall and wide with a mounded, dense growth habit. The lacey, fine-textured foliage is extremely effective in the garden long after the flowers have faded. A very tough species, showing both cold and heat tolerance in Zones 4–8.

Syringa Tinkerbelle ('Bailbelle') (Tinkerbelle lilac)

One of several introductions from the Bailey Nurseries' Fairytale series. Tinkerbelle exhibits a dwarf habit and deep pink spring flowers with a wonderful, spicy fragrance. The small, dark green leaves are the perfect backdrop to the beautiful flowers. These dwarf, floriferous bloomers are ideal for the home garden. A nice selection for cold climates. Hardy from Zones 3–7.

{ *Viburnum* spp.
Viburnum

Viburnums are without a doubt among the most versatile and enjoyable shrub groups available for the home landscape. There are literally hundreds of species and varieties that grace our natural woodlands as well as our cultivated landscapes. Many garden enthusiasts, growers, and horticultural experts agree that viburnums are the royalty of the woody plant kingdom. There are several reasons why such impressive accolades have been bestowed upon this exceptional group of plants. Viburnums are highly regarded because of their unmatched aesthetic value, ease of culture, and multipurpose function in the landscape. In most cases, viburnums will reliably offer multiple seasons of interest in the garden. They can provide vibrant and sometimes fragrant flowers, colorful fruit displays, dense growth habits, and beautiful foliage.

Viburnums are also adaptable to many climates in the United States. They are pest and disease resistant, drought tolerant, and will acclimate to most soils and light exposures. Ideally, viburnums thrive in moist, well-drained, acidic soils and full or partial sunlight. Viburnums also tolerate pruning very well and can easily be rejuvenated in early spring. To keep viburnums healthy and vigorous, regular selective pruning may be necessary to remove older, unproductive branches. Hardiness depends on specific species and varieties and can range from Zones 3–8.

Viburnums adapt well to a variety of landscape situations. They can be used as informal or formal hedges, screenings, barrier plantings, groups and mass plantings, specimens, and foundation plantings. In my garden, viburnum has earned the name "Old Reliable" because of its ability to perform unconditionally each year. It is truly a gardener's best friend.

Below is a list of common garden species and varieties that are ideal for the home landscape.

Viburnum x *bodnantense* 'Dawn' ('Dawn' viburnum)
This extremely fragrant viburnum displays small pink flowers at a time when most other shrubs are still dormant. I have witnessed it in bloom as early as January and as late as May in the northeastern United States. The deep pink flower clusters will open sporadically through the early spring when temperatures are not exceedingly cold. The upright growth habit and coarse branches make this plant a bold fixture in the landscape. However, this shrub can become rather awkward if left unpruned—I recommend you selectively prune older stems on a regular basis. This type of "maintenance" pruning will encourage vigorous and productive growth. Besides the showy, fragrant flowers, 'Dawn' viburnum also has deeply textured, rich green leaves during the summer months.

Since 'Dawn' viburnum offers delicate, fragrant flowers early in the season, it is valued as a specimen plant and often used in shrub borders and woodland gardens. When 'Dawn' viburnum blooms, it is usually

Korean spicebush flowers

a wake-up call that spring is just around the corner. Hardy from Zones 4–8, but should be sited in a protected location in Zone 4.

Viburnum carlesii (Korean spicebush viburnum)

This deciduous shrub has medium green leaves and a dense growth habit to 6–8 ft. in height with an equal spread. In mid spring the deep pink flower buds open to white, snowball-like flowers, which offer a potent, spicy fragrance. Fall foliage color is reddish purple but can vary from year to year. It is an excellent shrub in groupings and mass plantings, sited where the fragrance can be enjoyed. Hardy from Zones 4–8. 'Compacta' grows about half the size of the species, making it ideal for limited space.

Viburnum dentatum (arrowwood viburnum)

Arrowwood viburnum is a wonderful shrub native from eastern Canada to Minnesota and south to Georgia. It received its name from the Native Americans, who used the strong, stiff branches for making shafts for their arrows. As an ornamental shrub, arrowwood viburnum is often overlooked in landscapes, but it deserves more attention. It offers dark green, deeply serrated leaves, flat-topped, white flowers in spring or early summer and blackish blue clusters of fruit in the fall. Fall foliage color varies among individual plants but may range from yellow to a brilliant red or maroon. Arrowwood viburnum has an unmistakable presence in the landscape with a graceful, upright growth habit reaching 10–15 ft. tall with a similar spread. Although this plant needs space, it will add noticeable structure, or "bones," to the land-scape. This shrub will grow well in full sun or partial

Arrowwood viburnum in flower

shade and prefers adequate moisture and rich, well-drained soils. Arrowwood is one of the hardiest viburnums, growing from Zones 2–8. In Zone 2, it is best if sited in a sheltered location.

NOTABLE VARIETIES

In the past several years, some very good varieties of arrowwood viburnum have been developed. Here are a few exceptional selections:

Autumn Jazz ('Ralph Senior'). Graceful plant with yellow, orange, or burgundy fall foliage.

'Blue Muffin'. This dwarf selection has dark green, glossy leaves and clusters of brilliant blue fruit in late summer and early fall. Because it only reaches 5–7 ft. tall with an equal width, it is ideal for residential landscapes.

'Cardinal'. A terrific selection for the autumn garden with reliable bright red fall foliage color.

Chicago Lustre ('Synnestvedt'). This fast-growing, upright shrub has outstanding glossy foliage. An excellent selection to add rich texture to the landscape.

Northern Burgundy ('Morton'). Very graceful growth habit with early burgundy fall foliage color.

Viburnum bracteatum

This species is similar to *V. dentatum*. 'Emerald Luster' has dark, lustrous leaves, creamy white flowers, and clusters of blue fruit in fall. It is a superior selection, well worth inclusion in the home garden. This species is not as cold hardy as *V. dentatum* and can be grown from Zones 6–8.

Viburnum dilatatum (linden viburnum)

Linden viburnum is among the best viburnums for small, residential landscapes. They possess all of the ornamental virtues of many other viburnums but offer a manageable, shrubby growth habit and three seasons of interest. White, flat-topped flowers measure 3–5 in. across in mid spring and eventually transform into clusters of bright red, cranberry-like fruit in autumn. It is one of the best viburnums available for fall fruiting interest. During the summer, rounded leaves offer a rich green color and change to a deep red or maroon in the fall. Growth habit is upright and dense, reaching 8 ft. tall with a similar spread. Linden viburnum is suitable as a foundation planting, grouping, mass planting, in the woodland garden, or as a small specimen plant mixed in a perennial border. It grows best in Hardiness Zones 5–7 but will grow in Zones 4 and 8 in the right landscape situation.

Linden viburnum

Cranberry-like fruit of linden viburnum

Deep red fall foliage of doublefile viburnum

NOTABLE VARIETIES

'Asian Beauty'. The large, dark green leaves and bright red fruit offer a handsome contrast.

'Catskill'. Compact selection reaching 5–6 ft. in height.

'Erie'. A large-flowering selection, with flowers up to 6 in. across. Excellent fruit-bearing variety.

'Michael Dodge'. An unusual selection with yellow fruit. Very nice accent plant for the gardener who wants to introduce something different into the garden.

Viburnum plicatum var. *tomentosum* (doublefile viburnum)

One of the more popular and versatile viburnums for the home garden, doublefile viburnum inherited its name from the double row of white flowers that line up along the stems, like soldiers at attention. Flat, white, lacecap-like flowers emerge in mid spring and transform into deep red fruit in mid to late summer. This species is one of the first to display colorful fruit in the summer, and various species of birds will enjoy the fruit. The deeply ridged leaves provide wonderful texture during the summer and turn red or maroon in fall. Doublefile viburnum has a uniquely graceful growth habit, with the lateral branches typically growing in a horizontal arrangement. Once established, this shrub will become the focal point of the garden and make an impressive specimen. Best from Zones 5–7, but it will grow in Zone 8 with adequate moisture and specific siting.

Doublefile viburnum in a landscape

The dramatic flower and fruit of 'Summer Snowflake'

NOTABLE VARIETIES

'Molly Schroeder'. A new selection with pink flowers in spring and, if conditions permit, it will rebloom in the fall, providing another show.

'Mariesii'. An excellent, reliable performer with large, white flowers, beautiful red fruit, and superior red fall color. Its very noticeable horizontal branching habit distinguishes this plant from all of the others in the garden.

'Shasta'. A wide spreading selection, reaching 12 ft. wide and 6 ft. tall. Large, showy flowers, bright red fruit, and purple/maroon fall foliage coloration. A garden gem!

'Shoshoni'. Similar to 'Shasta', but on a smaller scale. It grows to 5 ft. in height, making it appropriate for small landscapes, perennial borders, and foundation plantings.

'Summer Snowflake'. A truly dwarf plant, reaching only 6 ft. tall and flowering continuously during the summer and into the autumn. It will flower heavily for the first few weeks and then bloom sporadically through the summer season. This is a very attractive plant that will also offer showy red fruit. Smaller in size and overall stature to most doublefile viburnum varieties.

Viburnum plicatum (Japanese snowball viburnum)

While the doublefile viburnum is undoubtedly a popular plant, Japanese snowball viburnum (the species from which the doublefile viburnum originated) can also be a beautiful addition to the garden. It is similar to the doublefile viburnum, but its flowers develop into rounded, pom-poms similar to a hydrangea's, but smaller. The growth habit tends to be more upright and less spreading, as well.

NOTABLE VARIETIES

'Grandiflorum'. An attractive shrub with noticeable horizontal branching habit, large white flowers, and beautiful green foliage.

'Kern's Pink'. The flowers are varying degrees of pink or white with pink tones.

'Mary Milton'. This unique shrub offers attractive soft pink flowers. New foliage growth in the spring is tinged with red, similar to 'Kern's Pink'.

Viburnum sieboldii (siebold viburnum)

There are several viburnum species that grow into large shrubs or small trees. One of the most popular species exhibiting this characteristic is the siebold viburnum. This large-scale plant adds a bold texture to the landscape with its large, oblong leaves. The leaves are a dark, lustrous green with very pronounced veins. Creamy white, flat-topped flowers emerge in mass at the ends of each branch in spring. The bright red, glossy fruit clusters ripen in late summer or early fall and provide an enjoyable meal for birds. The overall growth pattern is upright and dense at youth and eventually reaches 15–20 ft. high.

Siebold viburnum is an adaptable plant but prefers well-drained, moist soils and full sun or partial

Siebold viburnum in fruit

shade. It is an excellent small specimen tree for a home garden and also effective in mass plantings and as a screen. Hardy from Zones 4–8.

Viburnum opulus and *V. trilobum* (cranberrybush viburnum)

The American (*Viburnum trilobum*) and European (*Viburnum opulus*) cranberrybush viburnums are well known in gardens around the world. As the name suggests, they possess bright red, cranberry-like fruit in late summer and early fall. Fruit tend to have a translucent glow when ripe and will often persist through part of the winter. American cranberrybush viburnum has edible fruit that is sometimes used for jams and jellies. Cranberrybush viburnums tend to set fruit more reliably when planted in groups where they will cross-pollinate. With both species, white, flat-topped flowers emerge in spring en masse. The distinct foliage has three lobes and looks similar to a maple leaf.

Cranberrybush viburnum fruit

Foliage coloration in the autumn can range from yellow to deep red or maroon.

These dense, upright shrubs can grow to 12 ft. in height with a similar spread. For best flowering and fruit display, shrubs should be grown in full sun or partial shade. Cranberrybush viburnum prefers moist, well-drained soil but is very adaptable.

Cranberrybush viburnum is an excellent choice for woodland settings, mass plantings, backgrounds, and as screens. One effective way to distinguish these two species from other shrubs is to locate the suction-cup-like glands along the leaf stem. American cranberry-bush is best suited to grow from Zones 2–7, while its European counterpart grows from Zones 3–8.

NOTABLE EUROPEAN CRANBERRYBUSH VARIETIES

'Compactum'. A very fine variety, growing to only 6 ft. high and wide. It is an extremely dense plant with extraordinary fruit display in the fall. 'Compactum' is an excellent choice for the home garden, as this plant is more suitable for landscapes with limited space. Ideal in mass plantings, small groupings, and as foundation plantings. You will be the envy of the neighborhood!

'Nanum'. A low-growing selection, growing up to several feet tall with a similar spread. This shrub is not known as a heavily flowering or fruiting shrub, but it is grown because it offers dense growth habit and nice foliage. Perfect as a low hedge, edging plant, etc.

'Notcutt'. Large, white flowers and luscious red fruit. Excellent maroon fall color. This selection is has a reputation as a good performer and extremely showy plant in the landscape.

NOTABLE AMERICAN CRANBERRYBUSH VARIETIES

'Compactum'. A low-growing form with excellent, dense growth habit. Flowers and fruit are also very showy. Like the compact variety of the European cran-berrybush viburnum, this selection is very effective in small gardens or in areas with limited space. Also effective when used in combination with perennials.

'Wentworth'. Selected in the early 1900s for its larger, edible fruit. Fruit ripen in stages, starting with a yellow-red coloration and eventually aging to bright red.

{ *Vitex* spp.
Chastetree
Vitex agnus-castus (chastetree)

Chastetree is a summer-blooming shrub with fine, palm-shaped leaves and long spikes of violet blue flowers. The 12–18 in. long flowers will begin in midsummer and continue through early fall. The dark, grayish green foliage adds a beautiful, lacy texture to the garden as well. This shrub can grow 8–10 ft. tall or larger but can easily be kept in scale with annual rejuvenation pruning in early spring. Plants tend to get larger in southern gardens than in colder climates.

Chastetree in flower

Chastetree is a fast-growing shrub that prefers moist, well-drained soil and full sun. Plants are slow to leaf out in the spring but will flourish in hot weather. It thrives in hot, dry locations and is quite drought tolerant. Pruning is not necessary annually, but regular pruning will encourage masses of flowers and a dense, manageable growth habit. Shrubs can be cut down to 6–12 in. from the ground each spring and will grow several feet in one season.

Chastetree can be used very similarly to a butterfly bush in mass plantings or as an effective backdrop to perennials. This shrub will grow from Zones 6–9 but performs best in Zones 7 and 8.

NOTABLE VARIETIES

'Abbeville Blue'. An excellent selection with deep blue flowers.

'Alba'. This variety has attractive white flowers, providing a bright accent to the landscape.

Vitex rotundifolia (roundleaf vitex)

This dwarf species grows as a low, spreading shrub to 18 in. high and 5 ft. wide. The rounded, gray-green leaves and small, blue flowers provide a nice contrast in the landscape. It is suited for sunny, hot, dry locations in mass plantings, along rock walls, and edges of flowerbeds and is an excellent plant for landscapes near the seashore. Hardy from Zones 6–10. Some correspondence suggests that this plant will grow in Zone 6 and may get killed to the ground, though severely injured stems will likely resprout from the roots.

Humans aren't the only fans of the golden foliage of 'Rubidor' weigela.

'Red Prince' in flower

{ *Weigela florida*
Old-fashioned weigela

Weigela, like viburnum and hydrangea, is an "old-fash-ioned" shrub that is once again gaining in popularity. This easy-to-grow, floriferous shrub produces masses of small, pink, trumpet-like flowers in mid spring and sporadically through the growing season. This shrub typically grows 6 ft. high with an equal or greater spread and has graceful, arching branches that sweep down to the ground. The medium green leaves provide a nice backdrop to the showy flowers.

Weigela is not a particularly finicky garden inhabi-tant and will adapt to varying soils and light expo-sures. For best results, plant weigela in full sun and moist, well-drained garden soils. Pruning can be done several ways, depending on the desired outcome. To keep plants healthy and productive, occasional selec-tive pruning to remove older, mature stems should be done in early spring. If plants require pruning, some flowering will be sacrificed, but the following year plants will produce masses of blooms. If your shrubs are too overgrown or leggy, pruning shrubs down to 12 in. will rejuvenate them. If shaping or simple mainte-nance pruning is needed, wait until plants have finished flowering in spring before pruning them.

Weigela is a multipurpose flowering shrub that can be used much like forsythia and spirea. It is very effec-tive in mass plantings, groups, informal hedges, and foundation plantings. The more recent varieties listed below are excellent additions to the residential landscape, displaying improved foliage, flowers, and compact growth habits. Hardy from Zones 5–8 and possibly Zone 9 with adequate moisture and specific siting in a partially shaded location in the garden. The maroon-colored leaf varieties such as Wine and Roses will likely hold their leaf color better in cooler climates.

NOTABLE VARIETIES

Midnight Wine ('Elvera'). A low, compact variety to several feet tall with deep maroon leaves and bright pink flowers. This selection is very effective accent plant for a splash of color when mixed with perennials and other shrubs.

'Minuet'. This densely compact shrub grows 2–3 ft. tall with deep red flowers. The dark green leaves are tinged with purple for a nice foliage effect.

'Red Prince'. An upright growing shrub with cheery red blossoms that will reoccur much of the summer and into the fall.

'Rubidor'. The combination of bright yellow foliage and deep red flowers make this plant the neon sign of the garden. It is useful as an accent plant in a partially shaded are of the garden.

'Variegata'. A popular garden variety with pale yellow leaf edges and deep rose-colored flowers. This makes a very attractive accent plant in the garden.

Wine and Roses ('Alexandra'). This delightful variety has deep burgundy leaves similar in color to a fine red wine and rosy pink flowers that look like a bouquet of roses. The contrast between leaves and flowers is outstanding. Wine and Roses, 'Rubidor', and 'Variegata' can also be effectively used as cutback shrubs, which highlights their beautiful colored foliage.

Notable Evergreen Shrubs

4

Although this book primarily provides information on deciduous flowering shrubs, there are also many valuable flowering evergreens that can add beauty to the home garden. An evergreen is defined as plant that retains its leaves year-round. But it is important to note that even evergreens eventually lose their leaves. Most evergreens will retain their leaves for one to two years before shedding them as new leaves grow. Many gardeners prefer evergreens because they keep the landscape green, even during winter.

The list below presents many good flowering "broadleaf" evergreens, which are evergreen shrubs with wider leaves than needled evergreens. Please note that broadleaf evergreens require special care—specific requirements can be found in the chapter Site Selection and Plant Care, beginning on page 99.

Camellia spp.
Camellia

Camellia has an extensive, rich garden history and has long been admired as one of the most exotic and romantic flowering shrubs. During the eighteenth century, camellias were imported to Europe and America from Japan and China, where they grow in the higher elevations of the mountains. For many years they

Camellia flowers and foliage

were thought to be tender in cooler climates and only considered for greenhouse collections. But in several parts of the United States, such as the Southeast and the West Coast, camellias will grow outdoors. There are two main species valued as garden ornamentals in America. They are Japanese camellia (*Camellia japonica*) and Sasanqua camellia (*C. sasanqua*). These ornamental camellias are also close relatives to the tea plant (*C. sinensis*), a major economic crop that is used to manufacture tea. Camellia flowers are incredibly diverse, with many different flower colors and types to choose from. Flower colors range from white to pink to red and can even display two colors on the same flower. Camellia flower types can also vary from single to semi-double or double and can mimic the appearance of other flowers such as peonies and anemones. Equally striking is camellia foliage, which is a handsome, dark glossy green.

Camellias have specific cultural needs, similar to rhododendrons. They thrive in moist, well-drained, acidic soil with high organic content. Camellias also prefer light shade, and mulch will also help to protect their shallow root system. Although camellias thrive in moist, cool environments, they are remarkably tolerant of hot, humid conditions provided they are watered properly. Several pests, including scale and spider mites, bother camellias. If a pest problem occurs, take a sample to your local agricultural extension service for evaluation and suggested treatment.

Pruning to shape plants or to maintain dense habits can be done after flowering. If severe pruning is needed, wait until late winter or early spring, when shrubs are still dormant. This type of pruning will reduce flowering the first year but stimulate the plant to produce a healthy crop of flowers the next few years. In general, regular, excessive pruning should be avoided. Camellias can reach 8–12 ft. in height and 6–10 ft. wide but can be kept smaller with judicious pruning.

Camellias are excellent flowering shrubs to add structure and beauty to the home landscape. The long-lasting flowers, strong growth habit, and lustrous foliage offer great texture and vibrant colors in the garden. Camellias can be used in groupings and shade gardens and can also be utilized as informal hedges, screens, or individual specimens.

While camellias have traditionally been considered landscape favorites for warmer, moderated climates in the United States, extensive research has produced many new, cold hardy varieties that can be used in northern areas. The majority of these cold hardy selections are the result of extensive work done by two scientists, Dr. Ackerman and Dr. Parks. The Ackerman hybrids are primarily hybrids of several different species, while the Parks selections are hybrids and choice Japanese camellia varieties. These resilient shrubs flower in either fall or spring, depending on the variety chosen. The Japanese camellia varieties normally flower from early to late spring, and some of the hybrids bloom in late fall. In either case, camellias used outdoors in colder climates should be sited carefully and protected from cold, windy, and exposed areas of the garden.

One key element in successfully growing camellias is the time of year they are planted. To ensure your

Single-flowering Japanese camellia in bloom

camellia plants establish quickly, they should be planted at a time when weather conditions are mild and optimum for root growth. For example, in the North, camellias should be planted in spring after the harsh, cold winter temperatures have subsided. Plants will develop root and top growth during the spring and summer before the onset of the cold temperatures of autumn. In addition, camellias planted in these colder climates should be given north or west exposures to avoid morning sun in winter. If sited incorrectly, camellias are more susceptible to winter damage and leaf desiccation. The contrary is true of gardens in the South, where fall planting is recommended after the harsh heat of the summer has passed. In this situation, camellias planted in the fall in southern gardens will establish roots during the

cooler season before the scorching heat of summer approaches.

Although there are many fine hardy camellia selections available, here are a few garden-worthy varieties to begin your journey with this fine garden plant. The selections discussed below are most reliable in Hardiness Zones 7–9, although they will also grow in Zone 6 if properly sited.

Camellia japonica (Japanese camellia)
NOTABLE VARIETIES

'April Blush'. This variety grows into a bushy plant with deep green leaves and shell pink, semi-double blooms.

'April Rose'. This compact and rather slow-growing plant has rose-red double flowers. It is very floriferous and will bloom in mid spring.

'April Snow'. This relatively slow-growing plant has white double flowers. It provides a profuse display of color in spring.

'Kumasaka'. One of the oldest varieties of camellia, this variety has been grown in Japan since 1695. The double blooms are red or deep rose and open late in spring.

'Lady Clare'. This variety has semi-double pink flowers.

Camellia hybrids
NOTABLE VARIETIES

'Pink Icicle'. This hybrid has shell pink, peony-like flowers with early spring bloom. The dark green leaves tolerate winter sun and make a nice background for the large flowers.

'Polar Ice'. The white double flowers open in fall on upright branches. In ten years the plant will grow 6 ft. by 6 ft.

'Winter's Rose'. This dwarf camellia grows 3 ft. wide and 3–4 ft. tall. The pale pink, double flowers are produced in profusion in mid to late fall.

'Winter's Star'. Flowers are a reddish purple and emerge in mid to late fall.

Camellia sasanqua (Sasanqua camellia)

In addition to Japanese camellias and their hybrids, Sasanqua camellias can really brighten up the autumn with their wonderful white, pink, or red flowers. This species is generally smaller than Japanese camellia, growing 6–10 ft. tall. The plant has a finer texture than Japanese camellia does, with delicate flowers and glossy leaves. It is hardy from Zones 7–9 but should be protected in northern gardens. 'Cleopatra' is a very strong grower with pink, semi-double flowers and an upright habit.

{ Cotoneaster spp.
Evergreen cotoneaster
Cotoneaster dammeri (bearberry cotoneaster)

Bearberry cotoneaster is one of the easiest cotoneasters to grow in the landscape. It is very adaptable to various types of soil and light exposures, though it will thrive in well-drained, moist soils and full sun. While cotoneaster as a group is susceptible to some diseases and pests, bearberry cotoneaster is quite resilient to most of these problems. One devastating pest is lacebug, which is an insect that will feed on the leaves and can kill or severely damage plants if infestations are serious enough. Lacebug damage is easily detected by the small, white dots on the leaves, which create a white, hazy appearance.

Typically, bearberry cotoneaster will grow 1–2 ft. tall and spread up to 6 ft. Branches that touch the bare ground will often root, creating a colony of plant growth. The dark evergreen leaves turn a deep red or maroon during the winter months. Like most cotoneasters, the small, white flowers are somewhat inconspicuous, but the red, cranberry-like fruit are attractive.

This ground-hugging shrub is most effectively used as an edging plant, in groupings, in foundation plantings, and even for erosion control on slopes. Hardy from Zones 5–7 and possibly 8 in the right conditions.

NOTABLE VARIETIES

'Lowfast'. A popular variety that produces large quantities of fruit in the fall.

'Mooncreeper'. I have seen this plant growing in local gardens on several occasions and have been impressed with its appearance. It is truly a groundcover, staying within inches of the ground and displaying the best foliage of any cotoneaster available.

Cotoneaster salicifolius (willow cotoneaster)

The willow cotoneaster has long, slender willowlike evergreen leaves and a graceful, arching growth habit. This plant can reach 15 ft. in height but can be maintained as a smaller shrub with selective pruning. The flat-topped, white flowers offer spring interest, and the red fruit usually persist until winter. The textured, glossy leaves turn reddish maroon in fall and winter, providing multiple seasons of interest.

Willow cotoneaster performs best in full sun but tolerates partial shade. Although adaptable to varying types of soil and soil pH, this plant prefers well-drained, acidic soil. Prune only as needed since this species has a natural, graceful growth habit. Occasional selective pruning will keep plants in scale. As with other cotoneasters, a disease called fire blight can damage entire branches of this shrub. These infected stems should be removed immediately. Hardy from Zones 6–7.

Since willow cotoneaster is a large, upright shrub, the low-growing varieties listed below are more suitable for most home gardens.

NOTABLE VARIETIES

'Repens'. A low-growing selection with a weeping, graceful growth habit. Excellent red fruit ripen in the fall, and the foliage turns purple in winter. It may be semi-evergreen in extremely cold climates.

'Scarlet Leader'. This hardy, fast-growing groundcover is known for its beautiful green foliage that turns a deep purple in winter. White flowers transform into bright red fruit that ripens in late summer. This variety is a very vigorous and resilient plant, adaptable to many situations, growing on banks and slopes for erosion control or in rock gardens. It may also be trained vertically for wall espalier, which is a technique for training plants flat against a wall. Tolerant of exposed sites and alkaline soils, it matures to 12–18 in. tall, spreading 6 ft. wide.

Illicium floridanum
Florida anise-tree

This useful evergreen shrub has an upright, dense growth habit and reddish purple flowers in spring. The unusual, star-shaped flowers have many petals and transform into star-shaped fruit in the fall. This plant is not overpowering in the landscape, but provides subtle beauty that is enjoyed by the gardener who takes the time to observe the plant up close. Individual plants will grow 6–10 ft. or more in height with a similar spread, but usually less in colder climates.

This flowering shrub thrives in very moist, well-drained, organic soils and partial to full shade. Plants exposed to full sun will often turn sickly yellow or light green. Occasional maintenance pruning in early spring will keep this plant dense and compact.

Florida anise-tree, largely considered an ornamental for southern gardens, will grow in hardiness Zones 6–9. It is an excellent foliage plant for shade gardens, mass plantings, and screens. The leaves have a strong aromatic smell when bruised, and it is supposedly resistant to deer.

'Halley's Comet' is a floriferous selection with deep red flowers and dark green foliage. It is effective in groupings in shady areas of the garden.

Kalmia latifolia
Mountain laurel

Mountain laurel is a widespread native shrub growing from Canada to the Midwestern and southern United States. Although there are several species of laurel, the most common is *Kalmia latifolia*. This popular evergreen is the state flower of Connecticut and Pennsylvania.

In addition to its status as a highly coveted native, it is a highly cultivated ornamental, with dozens of varieties available for the home landscape. The use of mountain laurel as a valuable landscape ornamental in North America had generally not been widely accepted until the 1960s. Since then, extensive breeding has resulted in many new and improved varieties that offer a vast array or flower color, foliage appearance, and growth habit.

Mountain laurel has a great deal to offer the home gardener. This multistemmed evergreen shrub has dark green leaves, deeply textured brown bark, and round clusters of white, pink, or rose-colored flowers in mid spring. Some varieties offer a two-tone, banded coloration, which is very conspicuous in the garden. Close inspection of mountain laurel's flowers will reveal their rather unusual form. Each individual flower bud resembles a multifaceted star that bursts open to a bell-shaped flower. The flowers collectively create a fabulous display of color rivaled by few evergreen shrubs. The growth habit can vary among varieties, from 18 in. to 6 ft. or more with a similar spread. Older, mature native specimens can form a tall irregular branch pattern with twisted, gnarled trunks that can be very picturesque.

Mountain laurel is closely related to *Rhododendron* and has similar cultural requirements. However, once established, mountain laurel is quite drought tolerant and adapts well to changing environmental conditions. One reason for this is that mountain laurel has a very extensive root system that is capable of storing large amounts of water and nutrients. Mountain laurel requires drainage, and deep, loamy, or sandy loam soils are ideal. A light layer of mulch is also beneficial. In its native habitat, mountain laurel grows particularly well in partial shade and well-drained soils along hillsides. Garden varieties should given similar conditions, avoiding heavy, poorly drained soils. Mountain laurel prefers full sun or partial shade. Although mountain laurel has a slow to medium growth rate, it is well worth the time spent nurturing it.

Large, overgrown mountain laurels can be easily rejuvenated by severely pruning the plant in early spring down to about 12 in. Even tall, leggy plants with no visible growth at the base can be renewed. In addition to having an extensive root system, mountain laurel has hidden growth points called latent buds that will initiate once the plant is pruned. This type of pruning will create a compact, more manageable plant.

For many years, plant breeders have been working diligently to cultivate and promote mountain laurel as a viable garden plant. Because of its natural beauty, seasonal interest, and reasonable cultural requirements, mountain laurel has a lot to offer in the cultivated landscape. The evaluation and breeding programs of Dr. Richard Jaynes and other dedicated researchers have brought this plant to the forefront. Dr. Jaynes has been working on mountain laurel selections since the 1960s, introducing many new varieties to the trade.

Today, there are many exciting cultivated varieties of mountain laurel available, and the list keeps growing.

In general, these new varieties are more compact than the mountain laurels found growing in the wild. With such an impressive menu of noteworthy varieties, gardeners have almost any shape, color, and size to choose from.

Mountain laurel can be used in mass plantings or naturalized settings, small groupings, foundation plantings, screens, and informal hedges. Small, dwarf garden varieties such as 'Elf', 'Little Linda', and 'Minuet' are also effective in rock gardens and in combination with low-growing perennials. Hardy from Zones 4–9.

NOTABLE VARIETIES

The varieties listed below are a modest representation of available selections.

'Bullseye'. Creamy white flowers with a purple band.

'Carousel'. Showy, purplish banded flowers.

'Elf'. A compact grower with light pink buds that open to pure white flowers.

'Little Linda'. A miniature form with a dense, low, mounded habit and deep red flower buds that open to showy pink flowers.

'Minuet'. A dwarf grower with thin, glossy leaves. The pink buds open to flowers with a deep maroon band.

'Olympic Fire'. Offers deep red buds and vivid pink flowers.

'Raspberry Glow'. Deep red buds open to raspberry-pink flowers.

'Sarah'. The striking red flower buds open to large, deep pink flowers.

Kalmia latifolia 'Minuet' in flower

{ *Leucothoe fontanesiana*
Drooping leucothoe

Drooping leucothoe is a graceful evergreen shrub native to the mountains of the southeastern United States. The new growth of this shrub is bronzy purple or light green, maturing to dark, glossy green. The pointed leaves are alternately arranged along drooping stems. Individual plants will grow 3 ft. high and twice as wide and cascade down to the ground like a fountain. In spring, small, white, fragrant, urn-shaped flowers dangle from the bases of the leaves. With the arrival of winter, leaves change to purple until spring.

Drooping leucothoe is related to *Rhododendron* and likes moist, acidic, well-drained, organic soils. Partial shade is best for this plant, and full sun is only recommended if adequate watering and mulch is provided. Leucothoe performs best under the dappled shade of trees, where it is protected from harsh winds and exposure; however, it is also very tolerant of deep shade. Plants exposed to harsh conditions are more susceptible to leaf spots and other damaging diseases. Selective or renewal pruning should be done in early spring.

Leucothoe is very effective in shade gardens, mass plantings, and as a low screen and edging plant. It also works well in combination with shade-loving companion plants such as rhododendrons, dogwoods, and hostas. Hardy from Zones 5–8 and possibly Zone 4 with protection. In southern areas, this plant does best when growing in the coolest areas of the garden.

NOTABLE VARIETIES

'Girard's Rainbow'. Eye-catching marbled combinations of green, white, and pink in the leaves. A nice accent plant to liven up a shady area of the garden.

'Scarletta'. The new growth is a rich, glossy scarlet, maturing to deep green and eventually turning brilliant burgundy tones in winter. The growth habit is dense and compact, making it useful in the home landscape.

{ *Pieris japonica*
Japanese pieris

This popular evergreen is often incorrectly referred to as andromeda, which is actually an entirely separate group of groundcover plants. This common mistake is proof why the use of botanical names is the preferred way to distinguish plants. Japanese pieris has been used for decades as a flowering evergreen in residential landscapes. The small, hanging flower buds are obvious in winter and open to nodding bell-like flowers with a mild fragrance in spring. Since this plant blooms early in the season, the flowers tend be long lasting. There are also several pink flowering varieties that form clusters of noticeable pink or red flower buds in winter before opening in spring. The dark, glossy green leaves and rough brown bark of the stems are also fine ornamental traits. Japanese pieris can grow as high as 12 ft. but is normally considerably smaller, depending on the variety. Healthy, well-cared-for specimens will form dense masses of growth from 6–8 ft. in height in a small garden setting.

© Vincent A. Simeone

The red flower buds of Japanese pieris

This popular evergreen performs best in moist, well-drained, organic, and acidic soil and partial shade. Planting this shrub in full sun will result in yellow, bleached leaves and increased susceptibility to a damaging pest known as lacebug. Lacebug will cause small speckling of the leaves and can ruin the aesthetic value of the plant. Japanese pieris should only be pruned if needed. As with mountain laurel, overgrown or sparse plants can be rejuvenated by severely pruning plants to 12 in. in early spring. If severe pruning is not needed, selective pruning to remove older stems can also be done in spring. Selective pruning on a regular basis will help to maintain dense, well-developed specimens.

Japanese pieris is ideal in mass plantings, groupings, foundation plantings, shade gardens, as a screen, and is most effective when mixed with other woodland companion plants. Hardy from Zones 5–7 and will grow in Zone 4 with some shelter.

NOTABLE VARIETIES

'Cavatine'. A later-blooming dwarf form showing good cold hardiness.

'Dorothy Wycoff'. A dense-growing form with striking, dark red flower buds that open to pale pink flowers.

'Mountain Fire'. A white-flowering form with outstanding fiery red new foliage.

'Valley Valentine'. The dark green leaves provide a beautiful canvas for the rich maroon flower buds that open to deep pink flowers.

'Variegata'. A slow-growing, compact selection with white leaf edges and white flowers. An excellent choice as an accent foliage plant for a shady part of the garden.

{ *Prunus laurocerasus*
Cherry laurel

Cherry laurel is a dense, large evergreen with lustrous, dark green leaves and spikes of upright, white flowers in spring. Although the common name would suggest that is it is closely related to laurel, it is actually a relative of the ornamental flowering cherries. The straight species is not often seen in the nursery trade, but several widespread cultivated varieties of this species are useful in the home garden.

This shade-loving plant will perform very well in partial or dense shade. Plants benefit from some shade since full sun may cause leaves to turn pale green or yellowish. Cherry laurel also prefers moist, well-drained, acidic soil with organic matter.

Cherry laurel has glossy, dark green leaves and 2–5 in. long white flowers in spring that stand straight up along the stems. The variety 'Schipkaensis' is a common selection with thin, long leaves and a broad spreading growth habit. Plants can grow up to 5–6 ft. high and twice the spread. 'Otto Luyken' is a more compact variety, growing 3–4 ft. tall and 6–8 ft. wide. Excessive pruning should be avoided since it can ruin cherry laurel's layered, spreading growth habit. If pruning is needed, selective pruning in early spring or modest maintenance pruning after flowering is acceptable.

Both varieties are ideal as mass plantings or groupings in shady areas of the garden. They can also be effectively used as a low screen or informal hedge. This plant will flower well with no direct sunlight. Hardy from Zones 6–8.

{ *Rhododendron* spp.
Rhododendron

Rhododendrons and azaleas are among the most popular and varied flowering shrubs in the world. This group of evergreen and deciduous shrubs includes hundreds of species and thousands of cultivated varieties. Rhododendrons and azaleas are very closely related, with only a few physical differences separating them. Scientifically they both share the genus *Rhododendron*. *Rhododendron* is also within the classification of shrubs known as ericaceous plants. Ericaceous plants are in the heath family, which is a large group of flowering plants having similar physical traits and cultural requirements. For example, ericaceous plants thrive in moist, acidic, organic soils; partial or light shade; and cool conditions.

Rhododendron as a group also possess colorful flowers available in a vast array of colors and sizes from early to mid spring and extending into summer. They offer glossy, dark green leaves and a dense, upright and spreading growth habit that becomes refined with age. Rhododendrons and azaleas add bold textures and bright colors to the landscape and can serve many different garden functions.

For example, the yak, or yako, rhododendron (*Rhododendron yakushimanum*) is a Japanese native with a dense, compact growth habit and lush green leaves. The undersides of the leaves and new growth are covered with a felty coating called indumentum, which gives the entire shrub a soft texture. The flower buds are deep rosy pink, opening to a pale pink or white in mid spring. This species is used extensively in hybridization because of its cold hardiness and compact habit. It is perfect for the small garden with limited space and partial shade. Several varieties such as 'Yaku Princess' and 'Fantastica' are yak hybrids. This species performs best from Zones 5–7.

Rhododendron culture is very complex and can be a humbling experience for even the most experienced gardener. The key to successfully growing rhododendrons lies in a gardener's ability to provide them with a cool, moist, sheltered growing environment. As ericaceous plants, rhododendrons perform best in light, well-drained soils with good soil aeration and an sufficient supply of soil moisture during the summer. A soil high in organic matter or humus—

New leaves with indumentum on yak rhododendron

such as decayed leaves, pine needles, or other acidic compost—is preferable. Also, beware of using too much peat moss in your soils. A very fine grade of peat moss will hold too much water and will reduce soil aeration. A generous amount of compost incorporated into the soil at planting time, combined with mulch on the surface of the soil, will provide important nutritional elements and consistent water-holding capacity.

Rhododendrons and azaleas require acidic soil with a pH of about 5.5. Soils with a high pH can cause chlorosis, which is a yellowing of the leaves, brought on by a lack of iron or manganese in the soil. In this case, the soil will need to be acidified, which is explained on pages 99–100. Rhododendrons also need even soil moisture and are not particularly drought or heat tolerant. They have very shallow, fibrous root systems that are extremely vulnerable to moisture and temperature fluctuations.

Pruning can be kept to a minimum, although occasional selective pruning to remove older stems or shape the plant will ensure healthy and productive shrubs. Severe rejuvenation pruning can also be done, but this is not recommended on shrubs in poor health or on highly stressed plants. Any significant pruning on rhododendron should be done in early spring before flowering. One or more seasons of flowers may be sacrificed, but a strong, more compact, and more floriferous shrub will result. If only maintenance pruning is needed to keep plants tidy and well groomed, hand pruning can be done soon after flowers have faded. A technique called deadheading can also be done at this time, which is the removal of spent flowers or seed heads. This will allow the plant to put more energy into growth and next year's flowers.

In addition to possessing unique aesthetic value, rhododendrons offer many important landscape uses. They are very effective in mass plantings, shade gardens, as screens, and are highly prized for their rich color and bold texture. A rhododendron's beauty is maximized when its informal, natural growth habit is maintained. Highly exposed, windy locations should generally be avoided.

The rhododendrons and azaleas listed below are a small representation of the many good garden varieties available to the homeowner. These plants were selected for their hardiness, versatility, and overall aesthetic value. They are generally hardy from Zones 4–7, depending on the specific species or variety in question. Rhododendrons do best in cooler climates but may tolerate warmer climates and short periods of heat and humidity if well watered and sited correctly. At the end of each variety description, minimum hardiness zones are listed.

True Rhododendrons
SPECIES AND NOTABLE VARIETIES

'Aglo'. A medium-sized plant with light pink flowers and small, dark green leaves. Zone 4.

'Anita Gehnrich'. Showy deep pink flowers fade to pale pink. A nice mid-season bloomer. Zone 5.

'Capistrano'. Yellow rhododendron flowers are highly coveted by garden fanciers and hobbyists alike. This large, yellow-flowering variety blooms in mid spring. Zone 5.

'Fantastica' in flower

'PJM' rhododendron in flower

'Dora Amateis'. An excellent semi-dwarf plant covered with showy white flowers in spring. Dense green foliage makes it a perfect foundation plant. Zone 6.

'Fantastica'. A beautiful yak hybrid with bright pink flowers that glow in the spring landscape. Zone 5.

'Ken Janek'. A wonderful yak selection with a dwarf, mounded growth habit and soft pink flowers. The underside of the leaves has a soft, felty texture that adds a nice contrast to the leaves. Zone 5.

'Mary Fleming'. Creamy yellow flowers accented with salmon pink. Dark bronze foliage in winter. Zone 5.

'Percy Wiseman'. A beautiful, mounded shrub with flowers opening a light pink fading to creamy white. Zone 6.

'PJM'. An old standard—a small-leafed rhododendron with bright purple flowers and an upright growth habit. The glossy green, aromatic leaves turn deep maroon in the winter. Zone 4.

'Scintillation'. This variety offers large, attractive green foliage and showy clear pink flowers. Zone 5.

'Solidarity'. Elegant pink flowers with a light purplish pink throats. Plant habit is dense and mounded, becoming large and open over time. Zone 5.

'Taurus'. Gorgeous, large, deep red flowers glow against the deep green foliage. Before the flowers open,

Rhododendrons en masse

dark, purplish red flower buds offer winter interest. A real show stopper! Zone 6.

'Windbeam'. This small leaf variety has light pink flowers and a semi-dwarf growth habit. Zone 4.

'Yaku Princess'. Purplish pink flowers with a pale purplish pink blotch in the center. The attractive new foliage has a silvery appearance that matures to dark green. The undersides of the leaves also have a soft, cottony, dark orange-yellow coloration. A very compact, dense, rounded habit. Zone 5.

Azaleas

It is nearly impossible to truly appreciate the infinite number of varieties of azaleas that are available.

One can spend a lifetime studying colors, shapes, and sizes, trying to decide which one is best for their garden. The azaleas listed are a very small start to a large, overwhelming list of cultivated varieties.

NOTABLE VARIETIES

'Coral Bells'. A low-growing shrub with delicate, coral pink flowers. Zone 6.

'Gumpo Pink'. Pink ruffled flowers and a compact, flat growing shrub. Zone 6.

'Delaware Valley'. Clear white flowers with bright green leaves. 3–4 ft. high and wide. Zone 6.

'Girard Crimson'. Bright crimson flowers. 3 ft. high and 4 ft. wide. Sun to part shade. Zone 6.

'Girard Fuchsia'. Deep fuchsia flowers. Upright growing shrub will reach 3–4 ft. in height. Zone 6.

'Hino Crimson'. Brilliant red flowers and compact growth habit to 3 ft. high and wide. Excellent bronzy maroon winter color on leaves. Zone 5.

'Linda Stuart'. The flowers are a real eye catcher. The flowers emerge soft white with glowing, coral-orange edges. There is nothing else like it. Habit is low and spreading, 3 ft. wide and tall. Zone 5.

'Nancy of Robin Hill'. Light pink, semi-double flowers provide nice, bold color on this low-growing plant. Zone 6.

'Sherwood Red'. Dwarf plant with orange-red single flowers. Zone 6.

'Sir Robert'. Large, single, open-faced flowers varying from white to pink. A dense, compact semi-dwarf grower. Zone 6.

Rhododendron mucronulatum (Korean rhododendron)

A deciduous species, this is one of the first to bloom with purple flowers in early spring. The masses of flowers open before the leaves unfold, making it very visible in the landscape. 'Cornell Pink' has medium pink flowers. The rather open, upright growth habit will reach 4–8 ft. high with a similar spread. The fall color can be quite attractive, displaying shades of yellow to crimson red. Hardy from Zones 4–7. An excellent plant to group together with forsythia.

Rhododendron schlippenbachii (royal azalea)

An exquisite large shrub to 8 ft. tall with pale to rosy pink, fragrant flowers in mid spring. After the flowers finish, the newly formed light green leaves turn dark green before changing to brilliant shades of yellow, orange, and red in autumn. An excellent stand-alone shrub for a select area of the garden. Hardy from Zones 4–7, and best in cooler climates.

{ *Viburnum* spp.
Evergreen viburnums

Like the deciduous viburnums, evergreen viburnums offer function and beauty to the landscape. There are several species and varieties of evergreen viburnums that warrant serious attention. Evergreen viburnums offer superb leaf texture, dense growth habit, and interesting flowers. Because they are truly evergreen, these viburnums are very effective as screens, informal hedges, and in mass plantings. Below are a few types of evergreen viburnums suitable for the home landscape.

Viburnum × *burkwoodii* (Burkwood viburnum)

This semi-evergreen species has fragrant, white, ball-shaped flowers in spring and glossy, dark green leaves most of the year. It grows into an upright, open shrub reaching 8–10 ft. in height with a 6–8 ft. spread. In warmer climates it will usually remain evergreen, while in cold climates it may lose some or all of its leaves during the winter. Hardy from Zones 4–8. Protection from windy, exposed sites in Zone 4 is beneficial.

NOTABLE VARIETIES

'Conoy'. This is a truly dwarf variety with lustrous, glossy leaves and a dense growth habit, growing to 5–6 ft. in height with an equal spread. Because of its compact growth habit, this shrub is ideal for small landscapes and can be used in groupings, foundation plantings, or in a perennial border.

'Eskimo'. Large, white flowers lack fragrance but display a spectacular tableau of color in spring, with flower clusters reaching 4–5 in. in diameter.

'Mohawk'. This hybrid between Burkwood viburnum and Korean spicebush viburnum has a dense, rounded growth habit. Dark green, glossy leaves turn brilliant shades of orange, red, and purple in autumn. The red flower buds open to white, providing a sweet, spicy fragrance in spring. A real beauty!

Viburnum × *pragense* (Prague viburnum)

The Prague viburnum is one of the most beautiful and durable of all the evergreen viburnums. The dark green, glossy, and textured leaves provide interest in the

Prague viburnum in flower

Viburnum rhytidophyllum (leatherleaf viburnum)

Leatherleaf viburnum is the epitome of a broadleaf evergreen in the garden with large, leathery, dark green leaves reaching 6 in. or more in length. Leaves are noticeably rough with a sand paper like texture. The flat-topped, creamy white flower clusters in spring are also large, reaching 6–8 in. in diameter. Overall, the plant is large and coarse, growing to 15 ft. in height with a similar spread. Leatherleaf viburnum has an unmistakable presence in the landscape. Hardy from Zones 5–7.

A similar species, lantanaphyllum viburnum (*Viburnum* × *rhytidophylloides*) is a hybrid of leatherleaf viburnum. Lantanaphyllum offers a robust, dense growth habit, creamy white flowers, and reddish black glossy fruit in late summer and fall. There are several varieties that are quite impressive and very useful in the home landscape. Unlike leatherleaf viburnum, this shrub is not reliably evergreen and is usually semi-evergreen in warmer climates and deciduous in cold climates. Hardy from Zones 5–8 and Zone 4 in a sheltered area of the garden.

NOTABLE VARIETIES

'Alleghany'. Dark green, leathery leaves provide an excellent canvas for the white flowers in spring and bright red fruit that eventually turn black in fall.

'Willowwood'. Excellent durable foliage and arching, graceful growth habit.

garden all year. The flat-topped, creamy white flowers emerge in spring and will persist for several weeks. These shrubs can easily reach over 10 ft. tall with a similar spread, and occasional selective pruning will keep them dense. Because these hardy evergreens form a dense, rounded shape, Prague viburnums make excellent living screens, informal hedges, specimens, and background plants. The rich, glossy leaves also provide an effective accent in the landscape. Hardy from Zones 5–8.

Site Selection and Plant Care

The key to a successful garden is proper planning and selecting the right plant for your specific needs. A well-designed garden should be functional and aesthetically pleasing. By placing the right plant in the right place, many garden pitfalls can be avoided. Before selecting flowering shrubs, it is essential that gardeners understand some key factors about their landscape, such as soil type, light exposure, and climate changes. In addition, knowing the cultural requirements of your shrubs is vital to their success. Adequate soil moisture, pruning, fertilization, and proper planting procedures are all important aspects of gardening to consider. This section addresses many important components of garden maintenance and overall shrub care. By properly assessing growing conditions and understanding the needs of specific shrubs, gardeners can make sound decisions on selecting shrubs that will thrive in their garden. The proper care of flowering shrubs will result in healthy, productive, and beautiful plants that will offer years of enjoyment.

Soils

Garden soils can vary greatly in many areas of the United States. Soil textures can range from well-drained, loamy soils to heavy, clay soils to light, sandy soils.

These textures represent the soil's ability to retain moisture and nutrients. While most of the shrubs discussed in this book will perform best in moist, well-drained soil, there are some shrubs that need special conditions.

In addition to the texture of the soil, soil pH (acidity or alkalinity) is also an important factor. Certain plant groups, such as rhododendrons, prefer acidic soils while other flowering shrubs, such as lilacs, prefer neutral or alkaline soils. Soil pH is measured on a scale from 1 to 14 in which 7.0 is neutral. Soil pH that is below 7.0 is considered acidic, while soil pH that is above 7.0 is considered alkaline. Soil pH meters or test kits can be purchased in a local garden center or nursery and will allow you to obtain the pH of your garden soil. In addition, soil samples can be brought to your local extension service for testing. Soils can be manipulated by adding products to the soil to raise or lower the pH. For example, garden lime (calcium carbonate) can be added to soils to raise the pH, while incorporating products such as aluminum sulfate will acidify soils. However, only limited amounts of these products can be added to soil at one time, and soil pH should be altered gradually over an extended period of time. Natural products such as manure or compost will also generally acidify the soil.

It is essential that you test your soil pH and know what soil texture you have before planting. In addition to preparing for new plantings, soil testing may provide valuable information about existing shrubs that are not performing well in your landscape.

Proper Planting

In addition to knowing your soil conditions, it is imperative that proper planting techniques are used on newly planted or transplanted shrubs. It is not enough to simply dig a hole and place soil around the root ball of the plant. Special care must be taken to prepare the planting site. This planning will ensure that your valuable shrubs thrive in their new setting.

There are several important steps that should be followed when planting shrubs. Once you have selected your plants for an adequate location in the garden, the planting hole can be prepared. The size of the planting hole depends on the size of the root ball. When shrubs are purchased from a plant nursery, they are typically available as balled-and-burlapped (B&B) plants or in containers. Containers can range in size and type but are often made of plastic. Burlap is a cloth material that is used to cover and support the roots and soil of a plant for future planting in another location. In either case, the planting hole should be at least three times wider than the diameter of the root ball. This will allow the roots to establish in loose, fluffy soil.

It is very important that your shrub be placed at the proper depth in the soil. Shrubs that are planted too deeply are doomed for failure. The top of the root ball should be even or slightly above the soil level. In

Container-grown shrubs and balled-and-burlapped trees in a nursery

addition, all rope, plastic, wire, burlap, etc., must be removed for the plant to grow properly. Some burlap material may be treated with a product that inhibits it from decaying. This type of burlap, if left in the planting hole, may remain for many years. Therefore, any treated burlap should be cut out of the planting hole and discarded. This treated burlap often has a greenish coloration. In other cases, untreated burlap will naturally break down. As much burlap should be removed as possible, though leaving some in the planting hole is not much of a concern. At the time of purchase make sure to ask your nursery professional which type of burlap is on your plant.

Container-grown shrubs are handled quite differently than those that are balled and burlapped. Shrubs growing

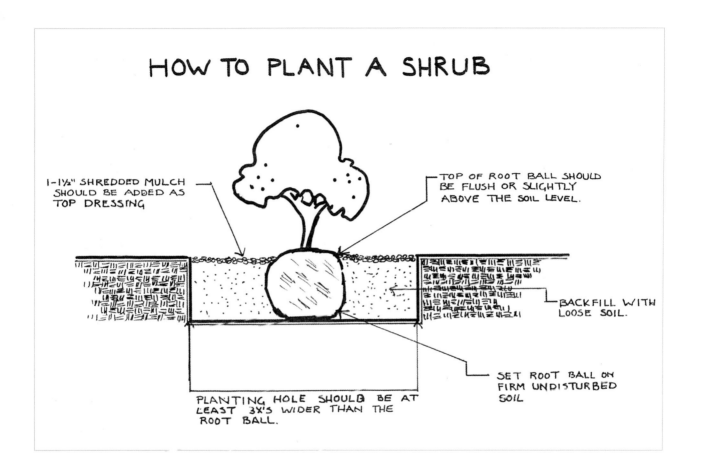

HOW TO PLANT A SHRUB

1-1½" SHREDDED MULCH SHOULD BE ADDED AS TOP DRESSING

TOP OF ROOT BALL SHOULD BE FLUSH OR SLIGHTLY ABOVE THE SOIL LEVEL.

BACKFILL WITH LOOSE SOIL.

SET ROOT BALL ON FIRM UNDISTURBED SOIL

PLANTING HOLE SHOULD BE AT LEAST 3X'S WIDER THAN THE ROOT BALL.

in containers are very often pot-bound, meaning that there is a large volume of roots that consume the container. As roots reach the edges of the inside of the pot, they form a thick mesh of roots. This fibrous web of roots should be carefully teased out or sliced with a knife to encourage roots to grow in the soil rather than in a circular pattern. This technique is especially important on shrubs with fine root systems, such as rhododendrons.

Regardless of whether your new shrubs arrive balled and burlapped or in containers, the planting procedure is similar. Once the planting hole has been prepared and the shrub is at the appropriate depth, soil can be backfilled into the planting hole and lightly tamped. Any excess soil, rocks, or other debris can be discarded. The shrub should be watered thoroughly and slowly so that the entire planting hole is evenly moist.

A thin layer of mulch covering the soil around the root ball will reduce soil moisture fluctuations and weed growth. Newly planted shrubs should be watered for at least two growing seasons to ensure they have established. The illustration on page 101 shows proper shrub planting techniques.

The best time to plant shrubs is in spring or fall while the air temperature is still cool and the soil is moist. Exact timing depends on the specific climate where you live and the species of shrub being planted. No planting should be done during the extremes of summer or winter.

Light Exposure

Light exposure in the garden, or how sunny or shady your garden is, also plays an important role in the success of shrubs. There are three basic types of natural light that can occur in the garden. Full sun, partial shade, or shade—with variations of each. Certain shrubs prefer full sun while others need some protection offered by overhead trees.

You can determine the type of light exposure in the garden by closely monitoring the sunlight during the growing season. This is generally best done in the middle of the summer season, when the sun is strongest. Areas of the garden that have at least five to six hours of direct sunlight during the day are considered full sun. There are different degrees of shade, from light to dense. However, partial shade is considered an area where plants receive shade for part of the day. Partially shaded gardens get about four hours or less of sun, either direct or indirect, per

An example of a partially shaded garden

day. In partial shade, if the plants do get direct sun, it is usually early or late in the day. Shade refers to an area of the garden with no direct sun or partial darkness.

Wind Exposure

In addition to light exposure, it is important to know the amount of wind your garden experiences. Certain shrubs will tolerate wind better than others. High wind exposure areas are usually found in coastal areas or seashore environments. In these cases, only a select group of plants that will tolerate these exposed conditions can be chosen.

Selecting the Right Plant for the Appropriate Location

Once you have determined the soil, light exposure, wind conditions, and any other important characteristics about the garden, other important issues must be addressed. The types of shrubs to be selected for the garden should be guided by several important factors. First, you must determine what you are hoping to accomplish when using shrubs in the garden. What is the desired function of the shrub? Do you need a mass planting for spring color? A grouping of shrubs to screen an unsightly view? Or a low planting near the foundation of your house to add interest? Also, what colors and textures are you interested in introducing into the garden? How will these new plants look with other existing plant material? And, most important, will the shrubs you have chosen outgrow the space you have selected for them? Putting a shrub in a location where it is sure to outgrow its space will only lead to problems in the future. Answering a few simple questions and taking some time to properly plan your garden planting project will most certainly ensure success.

Integrated Pest Management

Integrated pest management, or IPM, is a very important component of a garden maintenance program.

The main goal of IPM is to develop sustainable ways to manage pests and help people to use methods that minimize environmental, health, and economic risks. IPM incorporates many forms of pest control to effectively and efficiently control harmful pests in the garden. The main types of pest control in a successful IPM program include biological, cultural, physical or mechanical, and chemical controls, as well as proper plant selection.

Biological controls include the use of beneficial insects and other organisms in the garden. Several garden supply companies now offer beneficial insects for sale to release into the garden. While many of these beneficial organisms are common insects we can easily recognize, others are microscopic and harder to detect. One good example of effective beneficial insects that reduce harmful pest populations are ladybugs. Other beneficial insects include encarsia (a predatory wasp for whitefly), cryptolaemus (mealybug killer), and praying mantis. Biological controls have become very popular since it encourages the use of beneficial organisms to control pests without the need for pesticides.

Physical and mechanical controls are very similar and also require no chemicals. Harmful pests can be removed or killed by physically taking action. For example, pests such as scale can be wiped off very easily with a cloth and rubbing alcohol. Although this is very time consuming, it is also very safe to the plant and the environment. Mechanical control is similar to physical, but it usually involves some type of machinery. The use of tillers or plows to manage weed crops in an agricultural field is one good example. Many mechanical devices can be used with success to manage pests. Machines such as wood chippers are used to eliminate brush and wood, where beetles can live and breed.

Cultural practices are a very important component of IPM and usually relate to sanitation to reduce disease or insect problems. The main goal of reducing pest problems by using sound cultural practices is to create optimal environmental conditions for plants and to reduce plant stress. This will result in the reduced likelihood of plants being vulnerable to pest problems. In essence, the general theory is that healthy, thriving plants are less susceptible to diseases and insects.

One facet of IPM that can also be very effective is the use of new, genetically superior or pest-resistant plants. New varieties of landscape plants and agricultural crops are being developed on a regular basis. These plants are bred for pest resistance, drought tolerance, and improved aesthetic value. Many experts feel the use of these superior plants in the appropriate location will significantly reduce pest problems and the use of pesticides. Universities have plant evaluation and selection programs to evaluate plants for this purpose. The results from these programs are filtered down to farmers, nurserymen, retailers, and eventually homeowners.

The use of chemical controls such as pesticides is usually considered a last resort in an effective IPM program. Essentially, if all other reasonable means of control have failed or if there is no other choice, chemical control can be considered. IPM encourages alternatives to pesticides whenever possible. If pesticides are used to control pests, the safest, least harmful product to the environment should be considered first. Good examples of lower-toxicity pesticides are horticultural oils and soaps, which break down quickly in the environment with little residual. If a pest problem arises, be sure to contact your local agricultural extension service or horticultural professional for advice. Before applying any pesticides, it is imperative to read the label carefully.

The most important factor associated with IPM is monitoring the landscape. Gardeners must monitor the landscape on a regular basis to observe the quantities and types of pests that might be present. If low levels of pest populations are observed, no action may be necessary. Once pest populations reach a certain threshold or level of concern, it may be necessary to take action. One excellent way to monitor pest populations is the use of pest traps. Traps that are attractive to insects are used so that gardeners can pinpoint when the pest has arrived in the garden and then decide whether control is justified. With proper monitoring and implementation of sound pest management practices, landscapes can be maintained more efficiently and effectively. This creates a productive, safe, and aesthetically pleasing environment for all to enjoy.

Pruning

Proper pruning techniques are important to maintain the health and productivity of flowering shrubs. An ongoing pruning schedule will result in vigorous plants that will maximize flowering and fruiting potential. There are several factors that must be considered before pruning flowering shrubs. First, what is the species of the shrub? Second, what is the health of the shrub? (i.e., poor, fair, good, excellent). Third, what is the desired outcome? (i.e., hedge, naturalistic planting, specimen, etc).

The first question is important because you must first know the type of shrub you have before you can know how to prune it. In general, shrubs flower on two separate types of growth; new growth also known as current season's growth, and older growth, which is also known as previous season's growth. For example, common butterfly bush (*Buddleia davidii*) flowers on the most current season's growth. Therefore, it is recommended to prune these plants down to 6–12 in. each spring to encourage new growth, which will encourage more flowers. Removing dead flowers or light pruning can also be done during the growing season.

Shrubs that bloom on previous season's growth are pruned quite differently than ones that bloom on current season's growth. A good example of a shrub that blooms on previous season's growth is border forsythia (*Forsythia* × *intermedia*). Shrubs that bloom on previous season's growth can be pruned several ways. If shrubs are overgrown or not producing ample flowers due to poor vigor, selective pruning in the late winter or early spring while plants are still dormant will refurbish them. In this case, shrubs are selectively pruned by removing weak or unproductive stems and leaving vigorous, young stems. This technique may reduce flowering for one year, but shrubs will be stimulated and produce more flowers next year. This type of pruning will also keep shrubs in scale with their

surroundings. Another possibility is to lightly prune shrubs with a hand shear right after flowering. This will keep plants dense and beautiful without sacrificing too many flowers. This technique is typically performed on healthy, productive shrubs in need of shaping or grooming.

To adequately address the second question, the health of the shrub must be determined because plant vigor will influence the type and severity of the pruning. Plants in good health have a better chance of recovering from severe pruning than those in poor health do. However, proper pruning techniques can also re-energize older shrubs and improve plant health and aesthetics.

Question three is also very important since you must determine your goals and overall purpose for the shrubs you have selected. Knowing the function of these shrubs is essential in the types of pruning that will be needed to maintain them. For example, a shrub used as a screen may need different pruning than a shrub used as a hedge.

Types of Pruning

Several important types of pruning are described in detail below.

Selective pruning

Selective pruning is a method in which certain parts of the plant are selected and removed. For example, selective pruning may be necessary on a forsythia shrub that is not producing ample flowers. In this case the older, dead, or unproductive branches are selectively removed while younger, more vigorous branches are

Selective pruning involves removing older, unproductive branches (left); the result is on the right

Selective pruning can be done with a hand shear for smaller branches

left. Selective pruning can be performed on any flowering shrub, but it is particularly effective on shrubs that bloom on previous year's growth, such as forsythia and viburnum. A regular selective pruning program will benefit these shrubs greatly since it keeps plants productive and in scale with their surroundings. For best results, this selective pruning should be performed in late winter or early spring while shrubs are still dormant.

Rejuvenation pruning

In addition to selective pruning, rejuvenation pruning, also known as nonselective pruning, is important to maintain productive, vigorous shrubs. This type of pruning is drastic, but it will rejuvenate and stimulate shrubs. This method involves cutting the entire shrub down to the base or within 6–12 in. from the ground

The results of rejuvenation pruning; notice that all branches are trimmed to within 12 in.

in late winter or early spring when the plant is still dormant. This type of pruning will encourage growth from the base, or crown, of the shrub. Nonselective pruning is commonly done annually on shrubs that bloom on current season's growth such as butterfly bush (*Buddleia davidii*), hills of snow hydrangea (*Hydrangea arborescens*), and summer-blooming spireas such as bumald spirea (*Spiraea × bumalda*). Nonselective pruning can also stimulate shrubs that flower on previous year's growth, such as lilac and forsythia, but it will take the plant one or two years to recover and flower profusely. This is usually done when selective pruning is not a viable option.

Shearing

Shearing is a form of pruning that is done to maintain tight, formal shapes. In general, hand pruning shears or trimmers are used to prune off new growth and to keep the plant dense and evenly shaped. This type of pruning is not usually recommended since it is not optimum for plant health and can compromise flower and fruit production. Shearing will also cause little or no interior growth on the shrub since the outer layer of growth is so dense.

Pruning Broadleaf Evergreens

While the two types of pruning described above are typically performed on deciduous flowering shrubs, these pruning methods can also be done on evergreens. Mountain laurel, Japanese pieris, rhododendron, and other common flowering evergreens will respond to selective and rejuvenation pruning. After this pruning is completed, hidden buds along the stems will be activated in the spring. If evergreen shrubs are in poor or fair health, it may be necessary to selectively prune in stages to encourage new growth at the base.

Special care should be taken prior to any significant pruning. For example, shrubs should be fertilized in the fall in anticipation of a spring pruning. In addition, during spring and summer months after pruning, plants should be monitored and watered as needed to reduce possible stress. These efforts will encourage healthy, vigorous regrowth.

Timing

The best time to prune flowering shrubs is late winter or early spring, while shrubs are still dormant. Pruning at this time of year will reduce blooms on shrubs that

Mountain laurel with new growth one year after severe pruning

productive shrubs, yielding masses of beautiful flowers the second year. As for shrubs that bloom on current season's growth, such as St. John's wort and butterfly bush, new growth stimulated by pruning will yield many new flowers the same growing season.

While the best time to prune flowering shrubs is when they are dormant, some modest pruning can also be done during the growing season after flowering. You can use a hand pruning shear to shape or maintain a dense growth habit during the late spring or summer. Specific timing for this type of pruning depends on the species. It is important to note that only a small amount of growth should be removed after flowering while plants are growing in the spring and summer. As a general rule, less than a quarter of a plant's growth should be removed during the growing season. Hydrangeas are a good example of shrubs that are often pruned this way. If more than a quarter of the plant's growth must be removed at once, then wait until the plant is dormant.

No significant pruning is recommended during extended periods of extreme heat or drought, when plants are typically under stress. Pruning shrubs late in the season should also be avoided.

Tools

Proper pruning tools are essential in maintaining handsome shrubs that will produce loads of showy flowers. While there are many valuable tools that gardeners may use at any given time, none are more important than a hand pruning shear, lopping shear, and hand saw.

flower on previous season's growth. However, the plants will react positively to pruning at this time of year and will likely produce loads of flowers the next season. Pruning in this time period stimulates vigorous regrowth during the spring and summer. Although shrubs such as forsythia and viburnum may need a year to recover before flowering consistently, proper pruning will produce healthier, more

Essential pruning tools: hand saw (top), lopping shear (middle), and bypass hand shear (bottom)

A good hand pruner is one of the most important tools used to maintain healthy flowering shrubs. There are several types of handheld pruners, but a bypass type is the most appropriate. This type of pruner works like scissors and is effective because it will cleanly cut branches without crushing them.

Lopping shears are long-handled pruners that allow more leverage to cut larger branches than hand pruners. Handles can be made of metal, wood, or fiberglass, and the blades should also be the bypass type.

Handheld pruning saws are used to prune large branches that are typically too large for a lopping shear to cut. A sharp, thin saw will enable gardeners to effectively reach tight areas within a large mass of branches on a shrub.

All of the above tools must be kept sharp, clean, and well oiled. Regular maintenance should be performed to ensure proper effectiveness of these valuable tools. Failure to properly maintain tools may result in unnecessary damage to your shrubs.

Fertilization and Mulching

Most flowering shrubs will benefit from a spring and/or fall fertilization program using a general purpose garden fertilizer. There are many general purpose fertilizer products on the market, such as 10-6-4 or 5-10-5. In addition, organic compost products will improve the soil, provide natural fertilizer, and improve the water-holding capacity of the soil. Organic compost is organic material such as leaves or manure that has been aged to create humus. Humus is defined as a brown or black organic substance consisting of partially or wholly decayed vegetable or animal matter that provides nutrients for plants and increases the ability of soil to retain water. This humus is an excellent form of natural fertilizer that plants can readily use.

Organic fertilizer is one of the best ways to fertilize plants since it is environmentally friendly and is much less likely to damage plants, unlike conventional chemical fertilizers, which can damage plants if applied too heavily. In addition, compost incorporated into the soil when new shrubs are installed will help plants establish since it improves the water-holding capacity of the soil. Ideally, a balanced fertilization program incorporates several different forms of fertilizer at certain times during the year.

Mulching is generally recommended once a year depending on how fast the material decomposes.

The use of mulch on the surface of the soil around plants is also very beneficial. The best mulch products are natural organic material such as shredded leaves, wood chips, pine straw, or compost. A 1–2 in. layer of mulch will provide a cover of organic material, which will serve as a natural fertilizer as it decomposes. In addition, mulch will also benefit plants by helping to retain soil moisture, reduce weed growth, moderate extremes in soil temperatures, and protect plant roots. Certain plant groups, such as rhododendron, benefit greatly from the presence of mulch.

In addition to compost and other fertilizers, biostimulants are natural products containing beneficial bacteria and fungi. These biostimulants are applied or injected into the soil and assist plants in absorbing nutrients and minerals vital to plant growth. A healthy root system is very important for shrubs to establish and flower effectively.

Watering

Proper watering is crucial for flowering shrubs to thrive in the garden. Established plantings, although usually more drought tolerant and resilient than new plantings, benefit greatly from a consistent, proper watering regime, especially during extended periods of drought. Shrubs that are improperly watered or subject to severe fluctuations in the amount of moisture in the soil will usually not perform particularly well. In most cases, giving plants too much or not enough water will cause unwanted stress. Knowing how to properly apply the right amount of water to shrubs is essential and often challenging. Plant stress can compromise growth rate, flowering capability, and overall health of plants. In addition, stressed plants are usually more susceptible to pests and disease and severe damage or death may occur.

As a general rule, in climates where supplemental irrigation is required and in periods of drought, longer, infrequent watering is preferred over short, frequent watering. Specific watering amounts depend of soil types, water pressure, size of area to be irrigated, etc. For example, in the heat of the summer when plants are not receiving enough natural rainfall, watering shrubs for 2–4 hours once or twice a week will provide a deep watering. Deep watering will encourage the establishment of a healthy root system. In contrast, short, frequent watering such as irrigating five times a week for half an hour each time will only moisten the surface of the soil, creating plants with shallow, vulnerable root systems. Very often this type of watering will waste valuable water since much of it may evaporate in hot weather instead of penetrating the surface of the soil. Watering frequency is very dependent on climate, soil types, and plant species. Heavy, clay loam soils tend to dry out less often than sandy soils. Also, certain plant species thrive in high-moisture conditions, while others prefer, well-drained, drier conditions.

Unlike established plants, newly planted shrubs will require additional care for several years after planting. New shrubs should be watered consistently for at least the first two or three years after planting to ensure that they are properly established. This supplemental watering will allow the shrubs to develop well-formed root systems. In most cases, after several years these shrubs can then be incorporated into an ongoing irrigation schedule along with other established plantings in the garden. However, certain shrubs such as rhododendron and pieris may take longer to establish due to their fibrous, shallow root system. You should also consult with your local water authority on water restrictions for the specific community where you live.

Broadleaf Evergreens versus Deciduous Shrubs

In general, broadleaf evergreens require more constant soil moisture and tend to be more prone to desiccation than deciduous shrubs because of there large, lush, evergreen leaves. Since broadleaf evergreens such as rhododendron, mountain laurel, and camellia retain their leaves throughout the year, they are more susceptible to winter burn, wind damage, and drying out during the winter. In periods of heat or drought stress or severe cold temperatures, broadleaf evergreens will very often wilt. This wilting is a naturally occurring protective measure by the plant to reduce water loss through their leaves. Although deciduous shrubs can also be effected by heat and drought stress during the summer months, they are not usually susceptible to the same winter damage as evergreens since they shed their leaves in the fall.

During times of stress, anti-desiccants can be applied to evergreen shrubs. These anti-desiccants are applied to the leaves and will form a waxy, protective layer on the surface of the leaves to reduce water loss. This application is usually done during the late fall or early winter months, although some products can also be used in the summer. In areas subject to cold, severe winters, it may be necessary to apply anti-desiccants once in early winter and again during a mid or late winter thaw. It is important to consult your local county extension agent, garden center, or nursery professional before using these products. It is also very important that you read the label thoroughly before applying any of these products to your flowering shrubs. Wrapping broadleaf evergreens with burlap for the winter will also help to protect them.

Landscaping with Flowering Shrubs

While it is important to know the aesthetic value and growing requirements of flowering shrubs in the landscape, it is equally crucial to understand the function of these woody plants in the garden. Shrubs provide the "bones" of the landscape because they offer important structural and textural qualities that form the foundation of a well-designed garden. Throughout this book many landscape design terms have been discussed, such as utilizing shrubs as mass plantings, foundation plantings, specimens, and informal hedges. These terms are important to know and are described in detail in this section. Landscape design techniques are very complex and can be a challenging part of gardening. Landscape design is also essential to the success of gardening with flowering shrubs. Poorly sited plants with no intended design can become more of a burden than an asset.

The most common mistake made by home gardeners is not allocating enough room for their shrubs to grow. Misplaced or overcrowded shrubs will cause future

Plant combinations accent the summer landscape

problems in the landscape. This will also compromise the ornamental value and usefulness of these important woody plants.

A second miscue is planting shrubs with no real plan or intended purpose. Dropping a few shrubs randomly through the garden can create a confusing, unorganized, distracting landscape with limited effectiveness. Proper landscape design techniques can create continuity and excitement in the home landscape. The use of flowers, foliage colors and textures, textured bark, fruit, and interesting growth forms can all add great depth to any landscape design. The following list of terms are basic functions of flowering shrubs in the landscape.

Plant Uses

Accent: Accent plantings are attractive looking shrubs that will add interest to the garden. Accent plants can offer interesting bark, contrasting foliage, flowers, or fruit, and brighten up the landscape. An example would be using a variegated plant to liven up a shady area of the garden.

Background: Shrubs used as backdrops to other plants act as a canvas for interesting herbaceous plants and other woody plants. The structure and contrast that background plants provide enhance the entire feel of the garden.

Edging plant: Also called a facer plant. These terms refer to low-growing plants that should be placed in front of taller plants. Theses plants are an effective way to give a flower border definition and form.

Foundation planting: Foundation plantings are those shrubs used near or around the foundation of a house, building, or structure. The purpose of foundation plantings is to soften harsh architectural lines, and to create seasonal interest in a highly visible area of the living space.

Groupings: Groupings are strategically placed shrubs in small groups to accomplish a harmonious planting. If room is limited and a large quantity of shrubs are not necessary, a smaller grouping will maintain harmony on a smaller scale. Groupings in odd numbers such as three, five, or seven can provide a less formal, natural look.

Hedges, informal and formal: Shrubs used as hedges must have several important qualities. First, they must be low branched, multistemmed, and dense. Hedges are typically medium to fast growing and form a solid block of growth that can hide or enhance a view, depending on the need. Informal hedges are normally planted in straight rows or slightly off center, but the plants are allowed to grow in their natural form with little or no pruning. This results in a very graceful, pleasing mound of foliage, stems, flowers, and fruit, depending on the season. Formal hedges are planted in the same arrangement but are sheared consistently to create a very tight, formal appearance. This type of pruning will often result in a formal, dense wall of growth but reduced flower production.

Mass plantings: The use of one type of shrub in significant quantities will create harmony and maximize the effect these flowering plants can have in the landscape. Mass plantings are meant to create a natural rhythm that is pleasing to the eye and is often more attractive than one shrub planted by itself. Mass plantings are meant to be seen from a distance and can provide additional function as a barrier or living screen.

Screening: Shrubs used as screening plants function as a physical and visual barrier in the landscape. Their purpose is to hide a specific view, create privacy, or even act as a buffer to wind or noise. Evergreens or densely branched upright shrubs should be selected for this purpose and used en masse.

Specimen planting: A specimen plant typically refers to one individual plant that is very noticeable and is featured as a stand-alone plant in the landscape. These strategically placed shrubs are considered focal points or main attractions in the garden. In large gardens, several specimens may be clumped together to create a bolder impact.

Other Important Garden Terms

Compost: Compost is a rich, organic material comprised of humus and other organic material used to improve soil conditions.

Cultivated variety: A variation of a species that is produced through breeding or selection. Cultivated varieties, also called cultivars, are most often of garden origin.

Cutback shrub: A shrub that is severely pruned annually or every few years in early spring to promote new, vigorous vegetative growth and/or flowers.

Deciduous: Deciduous shrubs are plants that shed their leaves at the end of the growing season and regain them at the beginning of the next growing season in spring.

Dioecious: Male and female flowers confined to separate plants. Sumac is an example of a dioecious shrub.

Espalier: The method of training woody plants flat against a wall or other structure.

Evergreen: Evergreens are plants that retain their leaves year-round.

Groundcover: A low-growing, creeping plant that covers the grounds as it grows.

Humus: A naturally complex organic material made up of plant matter or animal manure.

Mulch: A layer of material, usually organic, applied to the soil surface to suppress weeds, retain soil moisture, moderate soil temperature, and add organic matter to the soil.

Soil pH: A measure of alkalinity or acidity of the soil. The pH is measured on a scale from 1–14, with 1 being the most acidic and 14 being the most alkaline. A pH reading of 7 is considered neutral.

Variegated foliage: Leaves striped, edged, or marked with a color different from the primary color of the leaf.

American Rhododendron Society
11 Pinecrest Dr.
Fortuna, CA 95540
www.rhododendron.org

American Azalea Society
1000 Moody Bridge Rd.
Cleveland, SC 29635-9789
www.azaleas.org

Broken Arrow Nursery
13 Broken Arrow Rd.
Hamden, CT 06518
www.brokenarrownursery.com

Camellia Forest Nursery
9701 Carrie Rd.
Chapel Hill, NC 27516
www.camforest.com

Collector's Nursery
16804 NE 102nd Ave.
Battle Ground, WA 98604
www.collectorsnursery.com

Completely Clematis
217 Argilla Rd.
Ipswich, MA 01938
www.clematisnursery.com

Cornell Cooperative Extension
www.cce.cornell.edu

Fairweather Gardens
P.O. Box 330
Greenwich, NJ 08323
www.fairweathergardens.com

Forest Farm
990 Tetherow Rd.
Williams, OR 97544
www.forestfarm.com

Gossler Farms
1200 Weaver Rd.
Springfield, OR 97478
www.gosslerfarms.com

Greer Gardens
1280 Good Pasture Island Rd.
Eugene, OR 97401
www.greergardens.com

Heronswood Nursery
7530 NE 288th St.
Kingston, WA 98346
www.heronswood.com

Niche Gardens
1111 Dawson Rd.
Chapel Hill, NC 27516
www.nichegdn.com

Rhododendron Species Foundation
P.O. Box 3798
Federal Way, WA 98063
www.rhodygarden.org

Rare Find Nursery
957 Patterson Rd.
Jackson, NJ 08527
www.rarefindnursery.com

Roslyn Nursery
211 Burrs Ln.
Dix Hills, NY 11746
www.roslynnursery.com

Song Sparrow Perennial Farm
13101 E. Rye Rd.
Avalon, WI 53505
www.songsparrow.com

Siskiyou Rare Plant Nursery
2825 Cummings Rd.
Medford, OR 97501
www.srpn.net

We-Du Nursery
2055 Polly Spout Rd.
Marion, NC 28752
www.we-du.com

Woodlanders
1128 Colleton Ave
Aiken, SC 29801
www.woodlanders.net

Yucca Do Nursery
P.O. Box 907
Hempstead, TX 77445
www.yuccado.com

Bibliography

In addition to the Web sites listed in Noteworthy Mail-order Nurseries and Helpful Web Sites, other Web sites and books were used in gathering the information for *Great Flowering Landscape Shrubs*.

Bailey Hortorium. *Hortus Third.* New York: Macmillan. New York. 1976.

Blume, James B. *Better Homes and Gardens New Complete Guide to Landscaping.* Des Moines, Iowa: Meredith. 2002.

Brickell, Christopher, and Robin White. "A Further Trio of New Daphne Hybrids." *The Daphne Society Newsletter.* Summer 2001. 6-14.

Brickell, Christopher, and Elvin McDonald. *The American Horticultural Society Encyclopedia of Gardening.* New York: Dorling Kindersley. 1994.

Cornell Cooperative Extension Nassau County. "Home Horticulture Fact Sheets." http://www.ccenassau.org/hort/html/fact_sheets_home_hort.html (accessed October 11, 2003).

Dave's Garden. "Garden Terms." http://davesgarden.com/terms/ (accessed September 9, 2004).

Dirr, Michael A. *Dirr's Hardy Trees and Shrubs.* Portland, Ore.: Timber Press. 1997.

———. *Manual of Woody Landscape Plants.* Champaign, Ill.: Stipes. 1998.

Fisher, Kathleen. November/December. "Cold Hardy Camellias." *The American Gardener.* Nov/Dec 2002. 39–43.

Feucht, J. R. 2002. "Evergreen Shrubs for Home Grounds." http://www.ext.colostate.edu/pubs/garden/07414.html (accessed October 18, 2003).

Fort Valley State University. "Crape Myrtle—Pruning." http://www.aginfo.fvsu.edu/teletips/trees/716.htm (accessed December 5, 2003).

Jaynes, Richard. *Kalmia: Mountain Laurel and Related Species.* Portland, Ore.: Timber Press. 1997.

Kelly, John. 1997. *The Hillier Gardener's Guide to Trees and Shrubs.* New York: Reader's Digest.

Meilland Star Rose Catalog. Cutler, Calif. 2004.

Murray, Marion. "A Whole New World of Hydrangeas." *People Places Plants Gardening Magazine.* http://www.ppplants.com/magazine/articles/articles_ma/4/4.html (accessed September 8, 2004).

New York State Department of Environmental Conservation and Cornell Community IPM Program. *IPM in and Around Your Home. Pest Management Information Series #2 Integrated Pest Management.* 1999.

North Carolina State University. "Roses." http://www.ces.ncsu.edu/depts/hort/consumer/factsheets/roses/roses.htm (accessed February 28, 2004).

Olkowski, W., H. Olkowski, and S. Darr. *Common Sense Pest Control.* Newtown, Conn.: Tauton. 1991.

Oregon State University, "Abelia 'Edward Goucher'." http://oregonstate.edu/dept/ldplants/abedw.htm (accessed September 8, 2004).

Plant Health Care Inc. Biostimulant information. http://www.planthealthcare.com/approach.html (accessed March 28, 2004).

Ritter, Francis. *The Royal Horticultural Society Shrubs and Climbers.* London: Dorling Kindersley. 1996.

Rakow, D. and R. Weir. Pruning: *An Illustrated Guide to Pruning Ornamental Trees and Shrubs.* 3rd edition. Ithaca, N.Y.: Cornell University Press. 1996.

Royal Horticultural Society Plant Finder. http://www.rhs.org.uk/rhsplantfinder/plantfinder.asp (accessed January 3, 2004).

Spring Meadow Nursery Catalog. Grand Haven, Mich. 2003–2004.

Street, John. *Rhododendrons.* Exeter, England: Justin Knowles. 1987.

Taylor, Norman. *Taylor's Guide to Shrubs.* Boston: Houghton Mifflin. 1987.

Virginia Camellia Society. "Very Cold Hardy Camellias." http://members.cox.net/vacs/cold_hardy.htm (accessed September 8, 2004).

Index of Scientific Plant Names

A

Abelia
    A. chinensis, 8–9
    A. × *grandiflora*, 7–8
Abeliophyllum distichum, 9
Aesculus parviflora, 9–10
Amelanchier, 10–11
    A. canadensis, 11
    A. × *grandiflora*, 11
    A. laevis, 11
Aronia
    A. arbutifolia, 11–12
    A. melanocarpa, 12

B

Buddleia, 12–14
    B. alternifolia, 14
    B. davidii, 12–14
    B. lindleyana, 14
    B. × *weyeriana*, 14

C

Callicarpa, 14–16
    C. bodinieri var. *giraldii*, 15, 16
    C. dichotoma, 15
    C. japonica, 15–16
Calycanthus floridus, 16, 17
Camellia, 83–86
    C. hybrids, 85–86
    C. japonica, 85
    C. sasanqua, 86
Caryopteris × *clandonensis*, 17
Ceanothus × *pallidus*, 17–18
Chaenomeles speciosa, 18
Chimonanthus praecox, 18–19
Clerodendrum trichotomum, 19
Clethra
    C. alnifolia, 20–21
    C. barbinervis, 21–22
Cornus
    C. alba, 23
    C. sanguinea, 23
    C. sericea, 22–23

Corylopsis
    C. pauciflora, 23–24
    C. spicata, 24
Cotinus coggygria, 24–25
Cotoneaster, 25–27
    C. adpressus, 26
    C. dammeri, 86
    C. horizontalis, 26–27
    C. salicifolius, 86–87
Cytisus
    C. × *praecox*, 28
    C. scoparius, 27–28

D

Daphne, 28–30
    D. × *burkwoodii*, 28–29
    D. odora, 29–30
    D. × *transatlantica*, 29
Deutzia, 30–32
    D. scabra, 31
    D. gracilis, 31–32
Diervilla sessilifolia, 32

Index of Common Plant Names

About the Collaborators

Vincent A. Simeone

Vincent has worked in the horticultural field for over seventeen years. He has degrees from Farmingdale State University, University of Georgia, and the C.W. Post Campus of Long Island University. Vincent has specialized expertise in woody plant identification, plant culture, landscape use, and selection of superior varieties of woody plants. Vincent is also an experienced lecturer, instructor, and horticultural consultant. He continues to promote innovative trends in gardening such as proper plant selection, four-season gardening, integrated pest management, historic landscape preservation, and low-maintenance gardening.

Vincent teaches a diverse assortment of gardening classes and has assisted in special garden tours to many beautiful gardens in southern England, northern France, southern Germany, New Zealand, and South Africa. Vincent is also very active in the community on local, regional, and national levels with garden clubs, horticultural trade associations, and public garden organizations. Vincent currently works in public horticulture managing Planting Fields Arboretum State Historic Park in Oyster Bay, New York.

Bruce Richard Curtis

Bruce has chronicled many of the significant events of the last decades of the twentieth century as a photographer for *Time*, *LIFE*, and *Sports Illustrated*. He has been on the front lines of the Vietnam War, covered the explorations of Jacques Cousteau, captured the glory of the Papal Archives, and chronicled the action on the fast-paced sports field.

His uncanny ability to capture the significant moment led Bruce to explore special effects with MIT physicist and Nobel laureate Dr. Harold Edgerton. His interest in action photography inspired Bruce to use pyrotechnics and laser light to create the "action still life," a combination of the best of special effects and still life photography in one dynamic image. The demand for his images in posters, calendars, books, greeting cards, and CD-ROMs continues to grow. Bruce's studio is located on Long Island, New York.